# MEN OF STEELE

## The story of Port Vale's stunning 1953/54 season

### By Phil Sherwin and the late Steve Askey

**First published by Pass Publishing in November 2013**

**Printed by Hanley Print, Unit 79 & 90, Bedford Street, Shelton, Stoke-on-Trent ST1 4PZ Tel 01782 280028/286358**

ISBN No   978-0-9926579-1-8

Acknowledgements;
Colin Askey
Gerard Austin
Brian Herbert
Dave Johnson
Eddie and Jean Jackson
Ray King
Dave Porter
Lindon Roberts
Smith Davis Press, who also designed and produced the Heroes of '54 booklet in 2004
The Sentinel

This publication could not have been completed without the help of Steve Askey, who sadly died suddenly on 17 September 2013, just a few weeks before it was due to be finished.

He worked tirelessly in helping to compile the information that was required, spending hours at Hanley library looking at Sentinels of the 1953/54 era on microfilm and then conscientiously writing it up, besides helping in many other ways.

He was a Vale supporter for 50 years, travelling to both home and away games and had a great memory of any games he had been to. He was a keen student of the history of the Vale, hence his eagerness to contribute to this book, about arguably the best season that the club have ever had. He was not related to the Vale player of the era, Colin Askey.

This book is therefore dedicated to the memory of Steve.

# Stephen Askey RIP

The statue of Roy Sproson which stands outside the main
entrance of Vale Park. This book tells the story of Roy's finest
hour in a Vale shirt

# Introduction

Men Of Steele. This is the story of Port Vale's tremendous season in 1953/54 when they won the Third Division (North) championship at a canter, setting records along the way, whilst also reaching the semi-finals of the FA Cup, being cruelly denied a place in the final by a former player.

Outside of the Potteries in Stoke-on-Trent, and it could be argued in some areas inside it, the name of Port Vale was not widely known. It was a popular question for football fans from all over the country – where is Port Vale?

During this season that all changed as they became extremely well known throughout the football world and beyond for their achievements on the field, with many people taking them and their achievements to heart.

They became the first English club side to play 54 competitive games in a season and apart from setting a plethora of records at league level they were only a hair's breadth away from becoming the first team from the third tier of English football to reach the FA Cup Final. 60 years later that goal still hasn't been achieved by any club at that level.

It was a romantic journey, taking place in a very different world to that which we know of today, which is also covered in depth in the book. Read how Vale were responsible for the start of the Berni Inns, suffered at the hands of Bill Shankly and turned down a blank cheque for one of their players. Read the story of a team of largely home-grown Potteries talent whose superstitions helped them to achieve their goal.

On the 60th anniversary of such a momentous campaign, this book details all the trials and tribulations every step along the way, also highlighting the way life was in those austere post-war times, when rationing was still around. Queen Elizabeth II had only recently been crowned, and footballers were limited to earning £20 a week. Yes, just £20.

# Life in 1953

Things in 1953 were quite a bit different from how they are today, both in football and life in general. Here are just some of the differences;

In football;

The maximum wage for footballers was £20 per week, irrespective of whether playing for Rochdale or Manchester United.
The British record transfer fee was £34,500, paid by Sheffield Wednesday to Notts County for Jackie Sewell.
Not many players had cars – just 4 of the Vale squad had cars in 1953/54.
Players didn't have agents.
There was no football and little other sport on Sundays.
There were no European competitions, no League Cup and no Football League Trophy, so the FA Cup was the only cup competition.
It was considered just as prestigious to be FA Cup winners as to be League Champions.
No substitutes were allowed, even if players were injured.
Goal average separated teams on the same points, calculated by dividing the goals scored by the goals conceded – simple!
There were no loan transfers allowed.
Foreign players in English football were very rare. 60 years later in the Premier League it is the English ones who are rare!
There were no floodlit Football League or FA Cup games, so midweek games had earlier kick off times.
There were no penalty shoot-outs; FA Cup ties had as many replays as were necessary.
The only televised football matches were the FA Cup final and the occasional England vs Scotland game. Football results were only announced on the radio, not the television.
If you missed the football results on the radio you had to wait until the newspapers came out to find out the scores.
There were no sponsors' or players' names on shirts and no squad numbers.

And on life in general;

There was no internet.
There were no mobile phones.
There were no motorways.
The population of the UK in 1953 was 50.8 million; in 2013 it is 64.2 million.
The Prime Minister was Sir Winston Churchill
UK currency was £-s-d: pounds, shillings and pence. 12 pence made a shilling and there were 20 shillings to a pound. In the book, where appropriate, prices have been converted to £ and p, rounded up to the nearest p.
Only 1 in 25 houses had a home telephone and 1 in 16 people owned a car.
Only 1 in 5 houses had a television. It was an even lower figure in the early 1950's but had increased rapidly because of the Queen's coronation in June 1953.
There was only one TV channel – what we now call BBC1 – and it was all in black and white. Programmes were limited to a few hours in the afternoon, then a break which was a blank screen, then a few hours in the evening, ending at around 10.30pm.
There was no advertising on TV, no teletext and no way of recording programmes.
There was no local radio.
The vast majority of photographs were in black and white.
All shops were closed on Sundays (except Oatcake shops of course)!
The minimum age to be allowed alcohol and to vote was 21. It remained that way until being lowered to 18 in 1969.
Pub opening hours were 11am -10pm, with a minimum 2 hour break in the afternoon. Most had longer than 2 hours.
Sunday pub opening hours were a maximum of 5 hours, usually lunchtime 12-2pm and evenings 7-10pm.

# Background

Port Vale are one of the oldest clubs in the Football League and began life back in 1876, probably as an offshoot of Porthill Victoria Cricket Club.

Their first games were played at Limekiln Lane, at the bottom of what is now called Scott Lidgett Road in Longport. They progressed enough to become one of the founder members of the Second Division of the Football League in 1892. By this time their home games were played at the Athletic Ground in Cobridge, the site of which is now covered by the Stadium Court Nursing home. They had also undergone a name change to Burslem Port Vale, the idea being to incorporate the name of the area into the club name.

It was a struggle at first. The team failed to gain re-election in 1896 but were voted back in two years later, mainly on the back of defeating First Division Sheffield United in the FA Cup. They were forced to resign in 1907 due to financial difficulties, and were effectively wound up, but the name was kept going by Cobridge Church FC, and in 1909 they were re-born as just Port Vale again.

The club moved grounds in 1913 to the Recreation Ground in Hanley, the site of which is under the car park of the present shopping centre. They regained their place in the Football League in October 1919 in unusual circumstances, being voted in to replace Leeds City, who had been expelled for making illegal payments.

Life was better in the Second Division this time around, up until they were relegated to Division Three (North) in 1929. They bounced straight back to win the championship at the first attempt though, and went on to finish 5th in Division Two in1930/31, still the club's highest ever placing.

In 1936 they were relegated again, this time to the Third Division (South), their geographical position meaning that they could be placed in either of the Third Divisions. New manager Warney Cresswell changed the club's first team colours to white shirts and black shorts, after previously being red and white.

Three years later the war delayed league football for seven years, by which time Vale had been forced to seek another ground, this time back in Burslem. Vale Park, as it came to be known, was opened in 1950, originally as the Wembley of the North with a ground capacity of 70,000, but that dream was watered down somewhat as money again had the final say.

Freddie Steele became the new manager in December 1951, and at the end of that season the club were moved from Division Three (South) to Division Three (North) at the request of the league, to permit Coventry and QPR, both relegated from Division 2, to play in the southern section.

In 1952/53 the Vale finished runners up, just one point behind Oldham Athletic, but in those days only one team was promoted.

Average home gates in 1952/53 were 14,504, the highest in the club's history up to that point and so hopes were high of a successful 1953/54 campaign.

Let the story unfold from there......

# Meet the Staff

**Freddie Steele (manager)**

Born 6 May 1916 in Stoke-on-Trent

As a player Freddie was a striker with Stoke City, for whom he scored what is still the record number of league goals in one season. He gained his first England cap at 19 and scored 8 goals in 6 games for them. In 1949 he became the player manager of Mansfield Town but couldn't resist the chance to return to his home city when Vale asked him to be their player manager in December 1951. In effect he negotiated the deal on his own, becoming the first player manager to transfer himself! He took the Vale to runners-up spot in 1952/53 and then the championship a year later.

Freddie remained as manager until resigning in January 1957 when the club were bottom of Division Two. He was re-appointed in October 1962, but it wasn't the same and he left by mutual consent in February 1965. He later became a publican and was landlord of the Plough Inn in Stoke.

He died at the age of 59 in Newcastle-under-Lyme on 23rd April 1976, three days before Vale celebrated their centenary with a game against his old club, Stoke City.

Vale appearances 25 Goals 12
Games as a manager 369, won 143, drew 105, and lost 121.

## Ken Fish (trainer)

Born 20 February 1914 in Cape Town, South Africa

Ken was the sergeant major type who took charge of the training. He gained four caps as a centre forward for South Africa and spent two seasons at Aston Villa. He caught the eye of the Vale when he scored all six goals against them in a match and signed for them three months later in 1937! A year later he joined Young Boys of Berne in Switzerland but returned to the Vale briefly in 1939. He then enlisted in the army during the war and served as a warrant officer.

He was a remedial specialist and chief PT instructor for a 2,500 capacity Field Convalescent Depot in France, Holland and Germany and was twice mentioned in dispatches. He became Vale's trainer on a full time basis in 1946 and was also masseur for Nottinghamshire County Cricket Club for three summer seasons.

He left Vale in March 1958 to become the trainer at Birmingham City. He later became the trainer and physio at Oxford United, a position he held for over 20 years until retiring at the age of 74 in 1988. He returned to the Vale for the Heroes of '54 dinner in 2004, but died on 4th August 2005, aged 91, in Stoke-on-Trent.

Vale appearances 6 Goals 1

14

# The Players

**Ray King (goalkeeper)**

Born 15 August 1924 in Warkworth, Northumberland

Ray began his career with Newcastle United and also played for Leyton Orient and Ashington before linking up with his brother George, a striker, at the Vale in May 1949. As a young player with Newcastle United he saved a penalty from Tommy Lawton at Goodison Park and, in doing so, broke both his wrists. Two years later he made a comeback with Leyton Orient and broke a wrist in his first game. In his next comeback he broke his jaw in his first game! Then his brother George persuaded him to come to Vale and make another comeback.

He was a regular for the first two seasons, but then dropped out of the side, being replaced by Ray Hancock. Another brother, Frank, was a goalkeeper with Everton.

Ray was transferred to Boston United for £2,500 in July 1957. He also managed them as well as Poole Town and Sittingbourne. He also set up a physiotherapy business (where his clients included a Liverpudlian by the name of John Lennon!), and occupied roles for Oxford United (coach), Luton Town and Southampton (scout). Nowadays Ray, aged 89, lives in Thailand with his son.

Vale appearances 275 Goals 0

**Stan Simpson Turner (full back)**

Born 21 October 1926 in Bucknall

In his first job Stan worked in a butcher's shop on Saturday afternoons. He then served in the army with the North Staffordshire regiment in India and was 22 years old when he joined the Vale in March 1949. He established himself in the team when Freddie Steele became manager. He began his career as a centre half, but preferred to play at full back. A tough-tackling defender, Stan did exactly what he was told to do to the letter and used to frighten left wingers to death!

Stan was transferred to Worcester City in July 1957. He later played for Burton Albion before becoming an insurance man in Stoke-on-Trent.

He died on 28th April 1991 in Bentilee aged 64.

Vale appearances 245 Goals 0

16

**Reg Potts (full back)**

Born 31 July 1927 in Etruria

Reg played for Stoke City and Northwood Mission before signing for the Vale in August 1945, making him the club's longest-serving player in 1953. Before he turned professional with the Vale he was a bricklayer. Initially national service, when he served in the navy as a sick berth attendant, disrupted his career but he became the club's regular left back in 1952. He was often the butt of player's jokes and was nicknamed Dan, after Desperate Dan, the cow pie eating strongman character in the Dandy comic.

Along with Stan Turner he was transferred to Worcester City in July 1957. Whilst there, he played in another famous FA Cup giant-killing act, when Worcester City beat Liverpool 2-1 in 1959. He later played for Macclesfield Town and coached schoolboys before ending his working life at Simplex in Blythe Bridge.

He died on 28th January 1996 in Hartshill aged 68.

Vale appearances 296 Goals 3

**Albert Thomas Mullard (half back)**

Born 22 November 1920 in Tamworth

Albert enlisted in the Royal Marines during the war but was captured by the Germans in Greece and held as a prisoner of war for four years until the war was over. He then began his career as a footballer with Hinckley United, Walsall, Crewe Alex and Stoke City. He signed for the Vale in Sept 1951 in exchange for Alan Martin, with £10,000 also coming to the Vale.

At first he played as an attacking inside right and was the club's leading scorer in 1951/52 but was moved to half back before the 1953/54 season. He was the only member of the Vale squad to have played in the top flight.

Albert left the Vale at the end of the 1955/56 season and joined Northwich Victoria. He ended his working life in the Wolverhampton area and lived near the football ground in Bilston.

He died of cancer on 27th May 1984 in Bilston, aged 63.

Vale appearances 178 Goals 23

## Tommy Cheadle (centre half)

Born 8 April 1919 in Stoke-on-Trent

Tommy worked at Mossfield Colliery and in the pottery industry before joining the army. Whilst there he was coached by Matt Busby, then a Liverpool player and he secured Tommy a trial there. In 1944, on a battlefield in Holland, Cheadle threw a faulty grenade, which went off almost in his hand. Tommy woke up in hospital where he met Ken Fish, PT instructor and Vale trainer. After being demobbed Tommy went to see Ken and got a trial at Vale, which led to him signing professional forms in May 1946.

Solid as a rock, he soon held down a regular place in the Vale defence and became captain. He was known as 'Wooden Head' because of his toughness.

Tommy joined Crewe Alex as player coach in July 1957. He hung up his boots at the age of 40 in 1959 and later became a postman in the Porthill area.

He died on 4th September 1993 in Bucknall aged 74. His legacy lives on by the name of the pub on the Hamil Road car park at Vale Park, Tommy's.

Vale appearances 358 Goals 14

**Roy Sproson (defender)**

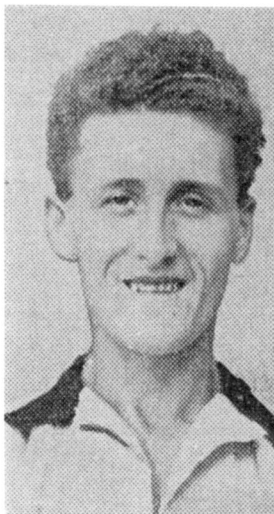

Born 23 September 1930 in Middleport.

A utility defender, Roy served in the RAF before signing for the Vale in July 1949 after being a junior with Stoke City. His brother Jess had played for the club during the war, and that swayed his change of allegiance. He became a regular in the side in 1951 and only missed one game in 1952/53 as they only conceded 35 goals all season.

Roy carried on as a player, winning the Fourth Division Championship in 1959, and was the club's first ever Player of the Year in 1967. He retired in 1972 after 22 years as a player at the time with the highest number of appearances in all competitions for one club, since being beaten by John Trollope and Ryan Giggs. He turned his hand first to coaching and was then made manager of the Vale between 1974 and 1977. After football, he ran a newsagents in Sneyd Green. He died in Stoke-on-Trent on 24th January 1997 aged 66.

His legacy lives on with Sproson Way and Sproson Park either side of Vale Park, and there is a superb statue outside the club's main entrance. Ironically, his nephew Phil is second on the all time list of Vale appearance makers.

Vale appearances 831+ 5 sub Goals 30

**Colin Askey (right winger)**

Born 3 October 1932 in Milton

Colin had played for Milton Youth club and graduated through the Vale juniors to turn professional in October 1949. His first few seasons were disrupted by national service in the RAF, but he became a regular towards the end of the 1952/53 campaign. He was a great crosser of the ball, could take defenders on and gave very consistent performances. Many, including Colin himself, said only a lack of real pace prevented him from playing in the top flight. Bred budgies as a hobby, and according to Ken Fish, he was about as big as two bricks!

Colin was sold to Walsall in July 1958 and after four years there moved to Mansfield Town. In 1964 he moved to Wellington Town and also played for Stafford Rangers, Winsford United, Macclesfield Town and Milton United. After his playing days were over he became an insurance man. Nowadays he lives in retirement in Milton aged 81, but besides watching the Vale he goes to Macclesfield Town, where his son John is the manager, and Newcastle Town, where his grandson James plays.

Vale appearances 217 Goals 23

**Albert George Leake (inside right)**

Born 17 April 1930 in Smallthorne

Albert began his career with Stoke City and also played for the RAF. He was good enough to play 6 times for England Youth and upon being demobbed he signed for the Vale in February 1950. His wages then were £7 a week plus £1 win bonus. He could also play half back and began to hold down a regular place midway through the 1952/53 campaign. He was also wicket keeper and batsman for Norton Cricket Club.

Albert stayed with the Vale, winning a Fourth Division Championship medal in 1959 as a central defender, until January 1961, when he moved to Macclesfield Town. Two years later he became their manager, but then worked as a School Attendance Officer between 1966 and 1995. He was also a decent cricketer, playing five times as an opening batsman for Staffordshire between 1955 and 1960.

He died on 24th July 1999 in Norton aged 69.

Vale appearances 291 Goals 43

## Carl Basil Hayward (centre forward)

Born 7 April 1928 in Leek

Basil was the brother of Blackpool centre half Eric Hayward. He was signed as a professional in May 1946, originally as a central defender, after a spell with Northwood Mission and a short stay in the police force. He became a regular defender in 1947, also playing at left back for a spell. Early in the 1952/53 season, Freddie Steele was injured and moved Basil up front as an emergency. He took to the new role like a duck to water and scored 22 goals, so Steele felt pleased enough to retire!

Basil reverted to centre half towards the end of his Vale career, which ended in July 1958 when he was sold to Portsmouth. Two years later he joined Yeovil Town as player manager, and also managed Bedford Town, Gillingham and Telford United. He then became chief scout at Norwich City, and had a further spell at Gillingham as a scout. An accomplished cricketer, he played 22 times for Staffordshire between 1951 and 1959 as a fast bowler.

He died in Stoke-on-Trent on 9th December 1989 aged 61.

Vale appearances 372 Goals 58

**Ken James Griffiths (inside left)**

Born 2 April 1930 in Bucknall

Ken began his career with Northwood Mission and after serving in the RAF during the war, joined the Vale as an amateur in 1945. As a schoolboy he played in goal, but soon found his niche at inside left. He turned professional in February 1950 making his debut a year later.

He was a regular in the engine room from the middle of the 1951/52 season onwards, helping the club to runners up spot in 1952/53 and the title a year later. He bred chickens as a hobby and had over 100 pullets so the team never ran short of eggs!

Ken was sold to Mansfield Town for a four-figure fee in January 1958. A year later he moved on to Stafford Rangers and also played for Wellington Town, Macclesfield Town, Northwich Victoria and Nantwich Town. He finished his working life as a storekeeper at Michelin, retiring in 1984.

He died on 9<sup>th</sup> August 2008 in Stoke-on-Trent aged 78.

Vale appearances 195 Goals 56

**John (Dickie) Cunliffe (left winger)**

Born 4 February 1930 in Wigan

Dickie, as he was universally known, began his career as a junior with Bolton Wanderers before signing for the Vale in December 1950. He also had a trial at Leeds United but was rejected for being too small at 5ft 5 ins. He only played a handful of games in the first couple of years, upping it to 19 appearances in 1952/53. He was a very skilful left winger, capable of giving defenders nightmares.

Dickie went on to win a Fourth Division Championship medal with the Vale in 1959 before moving across the city to join Stoke in September 1959 along with £2,000 in exchange for Peter Ford and Harry Oscroft. He only stayed for one season and then finished his playing days with Macclesfield Town, Stafford Rangers and Buxton. Afterwards he became a car mechanic, and was the landlord of the Cottage pub in Tunstall.

He died of cancer on 15th November 1975 in Tunstall aged just 45.

Vale appearances 302 Goals 55

**Derek Tomkinson (inside forward)**

Born 6 April 1931 in Stoke-on-Trent

Derek joined the Vale as an amateur in 1949 after his dad brought him to Vale Park one evening and said 'Could you give my boy a game?' He left in 1951 and went to play for Burton Albion. He came back to the Vale in December 1952 but was mainly used as a reserve.

The man whose only FA cup-tie was a semi-final, Derek was released on a free transfer at the end of the 1954/55 season. He then linked up with Crewe Alex for two years before ending his playing days with Macclesfield Town. He then became a company secretary in the pottery industry and worked at Keele University before emigrating to Spain, having also lived in France. He is presently 82 years of age.

Vale appearances 30 Goals 5

**Jim Elsby (defender)**

Born 1 August 1928 in Newcastle-under-Lyme

Jim was a full back who joined the Vale as an amateur in 1948 and turned professional in May 1949. He was a regular for the club's reserve side and had only made 5 appearances up to the start of the 1953/54 campaign. Jim ran a coach painting business as a sideline.

He left on a free transfer at the end of the 1954/55 season and joined Wereton Queens Park. His nephew Ian played for the Vale between 1978 and 1981.

He died on 7th September 1987 in Newcastle-under-Lyme aged 59.

Vale appearances 12 Goals 0

**Len Barber (forward)**

Born 3 July 1929 in Stoke-on-Trent

No relation to the club director of the same name, Len played for Bury before joining the Vale in June 1947. He was in and out of the side but did well towards the end of the 1950/51 season with 7 goals in 14 games. This could have been even better because he scored 4 goals against Crystal Palace in April 1951, only for the game to be abandoned with Vale leading 5-1!

Len left the Vale on a free transfer in July 1955 and joined Cheshire League side Northwich Victoria. He also played for Wellington Town. After ending his playing days he became the landlord of the Labour In Vain pub in Milton.

He died in Stoke-on-Trent in February 1988 aged 58.

Vale appearances 47 Goals 12

**Mick John Hulligan (winger)**

Born 28 February 1923 in Liverpool

Mick was a tricky winger who joined the Vale from Liverpool along with Stan Polk for a club record £10,000 in July 1948. A year later he was a regular member of the Vale side and was the only man to be ever present during the club's first season at Vale Park, 1950/51. He only missed one game in 1952/53 when the club came second in Division Three (North)

He was released on a free transfer in July 1955 and joined Northwich Victoria, along with Len Barber.

He died in Hartshill on 12th September 1978 aged 55.

Vale appearances 208 Goals 23

**Alan Bennett (left winger)**

Born 5 November 1931 in Hanley

Alan came through the club's junior ranks and made his debut aged 17. He turned professional in May 1949 and held down a regular place for the next three years. The emergence of Dickie Cunliffe though led to him losing his place during the 1952/53 season and he was just a reserve after that.

Alan left the Vale for Crewe Alex in September 1957 but less than 12 months later he announced his retirement from the game, aged just 27. He then first became a greengrocer and then a coal merchant and was also a very good ballroom dancer

He died on 17th January 2006 in Stoke-on-Trent aged 74.

Vale appearances 129 Goals 9

**Charles Ray Hancock (goalkeeper)**

Born 16 February 1925 in Stoke-on-Trent

Ray is actually his middle name. He played for Abbey Hulton United and Bury before he signed for the Vale in May 1948. He played 3 games in 1948/49 but then didn't play again until the 1952/53 season, when he only missed 3 games.

Ray continued to be an understudy to Ray King after that and left on a free transfer at the end of the 1955/56 season. He then linked up with Northwich Victoria. After his playing days were over he worked at Masons Textiles in Leek for many years His brother Ken also played in goal for the Vale between 1958 and 1964.

He died in Stoke-on-Trent on 20th April 2007 aged 82.

Vale appearances 52 Goals 0

**William Roy Brien (half back)**

Born 11 November 1930 in Stoke-on-Trent

Despite being christened William, he went under his middle name of Roy and signed for the Vale in May 1951. He was a regular for the reserves and was still awaiting his senior debut as the 1953/54 campaign began.

Roy made just the one appearance in that season, didn't add to it, and was released at the end of the 1954/55 campaign.

He died in Rochdale on 27th January 1987 aged 56.

Vale appearances 1 Goals 0


**Roland Lewis (forward)**

Born 21 September 1925 in Sandbach

Roland was a forward who played for Congleton Town before signing for the Vale in March 1950. A regular for the reserves, he was only used intermittently for the first team.

He was given a free transfer partway through the season in December 1953 and a month later he joined Witton Albion.

He died in South Cheshire in September 1999 aged 74.

Vale appearances 7 Goals 0

# The Boardroom

### Chairman – Frederick William Burgess

Born in Burslem 28 May 1888.

Fred was a master baker who established his own baking and confectionery firm. He joined the Vale board in 1944 and became chairman in August 1952.

He remained as chairman until August 1958 and then had a further stint as chairman for a year beginning in September 1959. His son John was also a director for many years.

Fred died in the Westlands on 4th September 1969 aged 81.

### Vice-chairman - Alderman William Arthur Holdcroft JP

Born in Ball Green 1883.

Founded WA Holdcroft & Sons Ltd, a musical instruments and furniture business in Brickhouse Street, Burslem. He was also Lord Mayor of Stoke-on-Trent in 1939. William was elected Vale chairman in July 1946, a role which he kept until August 1952, when he stepped down to vice-chairman.

William became the club president September 1954, taking over from the late Tom Flint.

He died in Stanfields on 8th July 1955 aged 72.

### Director - Jack Diffin

Born in Northern Ireland

Northern Irish international goalkeeper (1 cap) who also played for Belfast Celtic, Linfield, Shelbourne and Dartford. During his playing days he had a general drapery and boot merchants business in Belfast and established a road haulage business in England, as well as owning the Old Stone Spray Company in Stone with his brother.

He became manager of the Vale in 1944, lasting just the one year. Jack also joined the board in 1944, and became vice chairman in 1946, a position he held until 1952.

He remained as a director until December 1957.

### Director - Alderman George Leonard Barber

Born in Goldenhill on 9 October 1904.

He worked in the pottery industry before becoming managing director of a company that owned a group of local cinemas called Barber's Picture Palaces. He joined the Vale board in January 1950, being instrumental in the new ground development at Vale Park. He was the Lord Mayor for Stoke-on-Trent for1952/53, and deputy mayor in 53/54. He became a Justice of the Peace in December 1953.

Len was a fan of the club his whole life and became the life president in April 1981.

He died in Stoke-on-Trent on $2^{nd}$ May 2008, aged 103.


### Director - Joseph James Machin

Born in Middleport 1893

A Vale fan all of his life, he worked in the pottery industry and established his own firm, The Glass Pottery Co, general merchants in Tunstall. He joined the Vale board in January 1950.

He became chairman in 1961, but died in Stockton Brook on $6^{th}$ April 1963 whilst still in office


### Director - Wilfred Ernest Elkes

Wilf was the son of the founder of Elkes biscuits, based in Uttoxeter, and was the managing director of the firm. He joined the Vale board in November 1950.

He remained as a director longer than any of the others from 1953/54, leaving the board in September 1968

34

### Director - A.McMinn

Born in Tunstall.

He founded a bus company, later sold it and then after that, he restored a derelict pottery factory and began to manufacture ware, becoming the managing director. He joined the Vale board in 1949.
He left the board in December 1959.


### Director - LP Droy

He owned a company called Droys Cakes, which had a front page advert on Vale home programmes in the 1952/53 season. He became a director in March 1951, and was appointed chairman of the grounds committee.
He left the board at the end of the successful 1953/54 season.


### Director - Frederick Mercer Pinfold

Born in 1908.

He was the Chairman and managing director of Staffordshire Public Works in Glebe Street. He was elected to the Vale board in July 1953.
Fred became chairman in December 1965 and resigned from the board in March 1968.
He died in the Isle of Man on 6th July 1979

# August

After a successful 1952/53 season, manager Freddie Steele was rewarded with a new three-year contract.

Vale Park had a ground capacity of 42,000, which included just 1,010 seats. The main problem was a lack of cover, the only bit being a roof at the back of the Bycars End, which had been brought from the old ground in Hanley. 350 of the seats were at the back of the Bycars, but 578 were in the open on the Railway side of the ground (so-called because Burslem station was right behind it up until its closure in 1964).

**Burslem station in the 1950's**

The other 82 seats made up the Directors' Box on the Lorne Street side of the ground.

Plans were afoot to build a new stand on the Railway side of the ground, seating 4,500 and with covered terracing for 12,000 and stanchions had already been erected so that the work could start. The scheduled completion date was the beginning of the 1954/55 season and an appeal was put out for 3,000 tons of hardcore to help the building process.

There were Vale supporters clubs in Burslem, Hanley and Newcastle and season tickets cost the equivalent of £2.50 for the terraces and £4.50 for the few seats, and for the first time included reserve games.

36

Vale almost had King Herod on their books – not the biblical character but the surnames of two goalkeepers. Stoke City's Dennis Herod was on offer for £500, but despite holding talks, Vale decided against it and he signed for Stockport County instead. In the end no new signings were made, but four local lads were given their first professional contracts, Alf Jones, Selwyn Whalley (part time), Harry Oliver (part time) and John Poole (part time). Whalley was training to become a teacher, whilst Oliver and Poole were engineering apprentices. Don Bould and Ron Fitzgerald both returned from national service to become full-time professionals.

Altogether the playing staff consisted of 37 professionals, 21 full-time, 6 part-time and 10 combining playing with their national service duties. NB National Service applied to all men aged between 17 and 21, who had to serve a minimum of two years in one of the armed forces. It was increased from 18 months to two years in 1950. Sometimes players were still able to play games whilst on service, depending where they were stationed. The practice ended in December 1960.

The full list of professional players was;
Goalkeepers;
  Ray Hancock, Ray King, John Poole
Full backs;
  Don Bould, William Cook, Jim Elsby, Harry Oliver, Reg Potts, Stan Turner, F.Viggars*
Half backs;
  Roy Brien*, Tommy Cheadle, Ron Fitzgerald, Alf Jones*, Albert Leake, Derek Mountford, N.Rowe*, Roy Sproson, A.Wharton, Patrick Willdigg, Frank Wintle, K.Worrall*
Forwards;
  Colin Askey, Len Barber, Alan Bennett*, R.Bradshaw*, George Burrows*, Thomas Conway*, John (Dickie) Cunliffe, Ken Griffiths, Basil Hayward, Micky Hulligan, Roland Lewis, Albert Mullard, Stan Smith*, Derek Tomkinson, Selwyn Whalley
*Denotes players on national service.

The playing staff also consisted of 57 amateurs, the most notable ones being Harry Poole and Fred Donaldson, both of whom made a number of appearances for the first team, and Ken Higgs, whose career path took a different direction a few years later when he played cricket for Lancashire, Leicestershire and Test cricket for England.

The first team colours were white shirts, black shorts with black and white hooped socks. The change colours were red and white striped shirts, something that would never happen in the present day, being the long-standing colours of rivals Stoke City! The shorts were black though. The change shirts were donated by a businessman friend of one of the directors who was from the north east – Sunderland actually, hence the colours!

To assist him, manager Freddie Steele had a trainer called Ken Fish, a South African former Vale player.

The Vale players prepared for the new season in different ways. Goalkeeper Ray King worked as a builder's labourer, also turning down a full-time offer just before he was due to report back for training, whilst striker Basil Hayward played cricket for Norton and Staffordshire, right up to two weeks before the football season was due to begin. A more than decent fast medium pace bowler, Basil took 7-72 against Cheshire on 5 August before football took over for the winter months.

Locally born player Neil Franklin, the former Stoke and England defender who caused a stir by going to play in Colombia, was now back in England and playing for Hull City. He still lived in Stoke-on-Trent and was the licensee of the Bluebell pub in Hanley. He asked permission to train with the Vale in pre season but the request was refused as the club had introduced a new policy of not allowing players with other clubs to train with them as they had done in previous seasons. It wasn't just the Vale being awkward, Franklin's former club Stoke City also refused permission.

The players began their preparations for the new season and in a behind closed doors game the reserves beat the first team 1-0.

Thursday 13 August

The first (and only) public friendly took place at Vale Park with the Whites (first team) taking on the Reds (reserves), kick off 6pm (no floodlights in those days).

It was 5p to get in (10p in the seats) and all proceeds went to charity. The teams lined up as follows;

Whites – Hancock, Turner, Potts, Mullard, Cheadle, Sproson, Askey, Leake, Hayward, Griffiths, Hulligan

Reds – King, Wintle, Elsby, Mountford, Wharton, Brien, Barber, Whalley, Tomkinson, Cunliffe, Lewis

The reserves again sprang a surprise, winning 4-2. Derek Tomkinson pressed his claims for a first team spot following his release from the forces with a hat trick with Roland Lewis

scoring the other one. The goals for the red-faced whites were
scored by Basil Hayward and Micky Hulligan.

So that was the end of the build up – no new signings from other
clubs and only one friendly, and that was the first team against the
reserves! Contrast that with clubs' build up to a new season 60 years
later where they are almost forced to make signings and play up to
ten friendlies against other clubs.

**The two teams line up for the public practice game**

Training was taken by Ken Fish and Colin Askey recalled: "Ken
worked us hard; he was a fitness fanatic. He'd have us running from
Burslem to Hanley, into Northwood, across Birches Head into
Bagnall, then across Greenway Hall golf course. At that point we'd
stop at the Hollybush pub for half a shandy because we were all
knackered! Then we'd be off again, through Brown Edge, into Chell,
across High Lane and back to the ground. We'd had it by then and
couldn't get our breath.

At that point Ken would say: 'Right lads, let's get the ball out now
and have a game!'"

Roy Sproson said: "We were fit and trained hard under Ken
Fish, who always said that the Vale lads were the best he had ever
worked with."

When the fixtures for the new season were first published the season was due to start on Saturday 22 August and finish on Saturday 1 May, which was the same day as the FA Cup Final. The powers that be then decided to move the whole of the final day's programme to Wednesday 19 August to avoid a clash with the Cup Final. This meant that the Football League was going to start on a midweek date for the first and only ever time.

Wednesday 19 August

**Mansfield Town 1 Port Vale 2**

1953 was a happy period for the country, as Queen Elizabeth II had been crowned and Edmund Hillary had become the first man to climb Mount Everest. To add to that in a sporting context, in cricket England won the Ashes back from Australia for the first time in 19 years just over three hours before the Football League season was about to kick off.

For Vale's opening match at Mansfield Town that night, the Vale team was the same as that of the first team in the friendly with just two changes. One was in goal where Ray King replaced Ray Hancock, with hat trick hero Derek Tomkinson coming in for Albert Leake. Vale thought they had taken the lead after half an hour, but Colin Askey's goal was disallowed for a foul on the 'keeper by Basil Hayward. Mansfield went in front seven minutes after half time when Chris Marron breasted the ball home from a cross by Charlie Adam.

Vale levelled in the 69th minute when left half Roy Sproson was on hand to drive the ball home after a Derek Tomkinson cross had only been half cleared. Three minutes later Vale clinched the points when Hayward knocked home the rebound after an Askey shot had hit the bar. Vale held on to win, the only away win in the division that evening.

Vale – King, Turner, Potts, Mullard, Cheadle, Sproson, Askey, Tomkinson, Hayward, Griffiths, Hulligan
Att 10,410

Colin Askey said, "Ray Hancock was very unlucky. He had been in goal for almost all of the previous season when we only missed promotion by one point but Freddie Steele decided to bring Ray King in after the Possibles v Probables pre-season friendly. Results were largely good from then on and Hanc couldn't get his place back."

The club held its AGM to bask in the glory of the profit of £1,676 on the previous season. President Tom Flint was ill and confined to bed.

## Saturday 22 August

**Port Vale 0 Barnsley 0**

Over 14,000 fans turned up but went home disappointed, as the Valiants couldn't break down a resolute Barnsley rearguard. Hayward and Micky Hulligan both went close but there was nothing doing as any chances all went begging.

Vale – King, Turner, Potts, Mullard, Cheadle, Sproson, Askey, Tomkinson, Hayward, Griffiths, Hulligan
Att 14,223

Colin Askey's brother Ray was taken on as a junior at the Vale.

## Monday 24 August

**Barrow 0 Port Vale 0**

There was no rest as two days after the Barnsley game Vale made the long trip to Barrow. Albert Leake came into the side for Derek Tomkinson and Dickie Cunliffe replaced Micky Hulligan on the left wing in the team's only changes. The game was played on a poor pitch with a low sun, so playing football wasn't easy. In the 5th minute Hayward hit a shot that home 'keeper Jack Hindle turned round the post, but that was the closest Vale came to a goal. Askey was a constant threat and Ken Griffiths broke clear of the offside trap only to loft his shot over the bar. At the other end Barrow hit the bar, but it would have been an undeserved victory.

Vale – King, Turner, Potts, Mullard, Cheadle, Sproson, Askey, Leake, Hayward, Griffiths, Cunliffe
Att 7,783

Roy Sproson said: "Barrow had a player who lived in Preston and he travelled up with us on the train. Sitting in our compartment, he told us that even at that early stage of the season he was going to have £25 on us to win the championship!"

<u>Saturday 29 August</u>

**Darlington 0 Port Vale 3**

In a busy start to the season, Vale were on the road again, this time to Darlington. The game was at Feethams and on the same afternoon cricket was being played next door and the press box had a perfect view of both games! Frequent showers made the scribes stick to football though, which in turn was played on a very wet surface. Vale went in front in the 27th minute when Askey flighted his centre to the far top angle of the Darlington goal and Hayward headed it down and into the net. Soon afterwards the Quakers almost levelled when Les Robson hit a screamer that Ray King pushed onto the bar only for Jim Scarborough to hook the ball over the gaping net.

Ken Griffiths scored twice within three minutes in the last ten minutes of the second half to wrap up the points and send the Vale to the top of the league. First of all Hayward broke away along the right wing and cut in before slipping the ball across to Griffiths who beat goalkeeper Billy Dunn with a first time shot. Then, from another pass by Hayward, Griffiths took the ball down the middle, went past Dunn and ran on to shoot into an empty net.

Vale – King, Turner, Potts, Mullard, Cheadle, Sproson, Askey, Leake, Hayward, Griffiths, Cunliffe
Att 6,278

<u>Monday 31 August</u>

**Port Vale 4 Barrow 0**

Vale entertained Barrow who included three brothers all playing on the left hand side: Jack Keen at left half, Alan Keen at inside left and Bert Keen on the left wing! The only previous instance of three brothers in the same league team were Jack, William and George Carr, for Middlesbrough in 1920. It has only been equalled on one other occasion, when Danny, Rod and Ray Wallace played for Southampton in 1988.

After 11 minutes Vale went in front when Albert Leake slipped the ball through to Basil Hayward who pulled it back for Griffiths to flash a drive well out of Barrow goalkeeper Jack Hindle's reach. Hayward made it 2-0 on the half-hour, shooting into the corner of the net after a long solo run. In the first minute of the second half Cunliffe passed to Griffiths who squared the ball to Hayward and he gave the 'keeper no chance. The scoring was completed when, eight minutes from time, Askey beat Jack Keen to the ball and centred for Hayward to complete his hat-trick with a header.

Vale – King, Turner, Potts, Mullard, Cheadle, Sproson, Askey, Leake, Hayward, Griffiths, Cunliffe
Att 13,403

Colin Askey said: "Eight of the first eleven were Potteries lads from similar working-class backgrounds. Vale scoured the local area, looking for players and listening about players. Local lads were signed and came through the ranks so we had known each other for a good while and there was a good atmosphere."
He continued: "The majority of our players didn't have a car; we would join supporters on PMT buses to get to home games. I would get on the bus at Milton, and we'd pick up Ken Griffiths and Ray Hancock at Abbey Hulton. Stan Turner and Reg Potts would get on the bus before we changed at Hanley. Roy Sproson got the bus in to Hanley from Hanford, so then we'd all get into Burslem on the bus with the supporters."

League table
(top 6) :

|  | P | W | D | L | F | A | PTS |
|---|---|---|---|---|---|---|---|
| PORT VALE | 5 | 3 | 2 | 0 | 9 | 1 | 8 |
| Gateshead | 4 | 2 | 2 | 0 | 6 | 3 | 6 |
| Mansfield T | 5 | 2 | 2 | 1 | 11 | 7 | 6 |
| Crewe Alex | 5 | 1 | 4 | 0 | 4 | 3 | 6 |
| Stockport Co | 5 | 2 | 2 | 1 | 7 | 6 | 6 |
| Chesterfield | 5 | 2 | 2 | 1 | 5 | 5 | 6 |

# September

In September, Selwyn Whalley was called up for National Service. George Burrows, Stan Smith and Roy Brien were demobbed and became full professionals.

<u>Saturday 5 September</u>

**Port Vale 3 Hartlepools United 1**

After the convincing win over Barrow, over 20,000 flocked to Vale Park for the match against Hartlepools United which opened with a flurry of goals, beginning when Vale took the lead courtesy of another goal from Basil Hayward in only the second minute. Tommy Cheadle's clearance to Albert Mullard was slipped to Hayward who scored with a left foot shot. Hartlepools equalised after 18 minutes when, following a Tommy McGuigan shot, the ball ran to Billy Burnett who promptly drove it into the corner of the net. Hayward restored Vale's lead a minute later, heading home an Askey cross. Ken Griffiths made it 3-1 two minutes after that when he took a pass from Leake, rounded the advancing goalkeeper and shot into the net before defender Joe Willetts could intervene.

Vale – King, Turner, Potts, Mullard, Cheadle, Sproson, Askey, Leake, Hayward, Griffiths, Cunliffe
Att 20,052

<u>Monday 7 September</u>

**Port Vale 2 Bradford Park Avenue 0**

The encounter with Bradford Park Avenue the following Monday kicked off at 6pm.
After ten minutes of the game, Ken Griffiths cut through on the left and his cross eluded Bradford 'keeper Mitch Downie and rebounded off the bar. As it fell Albert Leake nodded it into the net. In the 24th minute Askey centred for Hayward to head down to Leake, who quickly flashed the ball home for his second goal of the game.

Bradford had James Milburn in their team, cousin of Newcastle United's more famous Jackie Milburn.

Vale – King, Turner, Potts, Mullard, Cheadle, Sproson, Askey, Leake, Hayward, Griffiths, Cunliffe
Att 19,270

Albert Leake said, "During the season players had to be in their own homes by 10 o'clock at night from Wednesday onwards. One Thursday I attended the annual dinner dance for Norton Cricket Club, who I played for during the summer, but my wife wasn't pleased when Freddie Steele told me to go home after the meal had finished!"

**Albert Leake scores the first goal against Bradford PA**

Saturday 12 September

**Gateshead 1 Port Vale 0**

The following Saturday Vale travelled to Redheugh Park to play Gateshead in what promised to be a much tougher game. Vale played in red and white stripes as Gateshead's colours were white shirts and black shorts and a 57$^{th}$ minute goal from John Ingham secured the points for the home side in a tight contest. Ken Smith drew the Vale defence before slipping a pass to Les Price who centred for Ingham to beat King. It was Vale's first defeat of the season and ended the club's record run at the time of 16 games without defeat. Although Vale remained at the top of the table, it was now only on goal average from Crewe and Bradford City.

Vale – King, Turner, Potts, Mullard, Cheadle, Sproson, Askey, Leake, Hayward, Griffiths, Cunliffe
Att 11,382

On the same day, Nikita Khrushchev became the Soviet leader, six months after the death of Joseph Stalin.

During the course of the 1952/53 season, the club flag over the Hamil Road entrance was withdrawn because of its tattered state and was replaced by an old style but better conditioned red one, a relic of the days when the team wore red shirts. But now a black and white flag was restored, made during the summer months by Mr and Mrs Hewitt and their daughter, whose Bycars Farm was adjacent to Vale Park.

Dr E.F. Higgins, honorary club doctor to the Vale for many years, retired from private practice but decided to continue to serve the club in an advisory capacity for which he was not paid. He had been the club doctor since 1925, a role he continued to fulfil until December 1956.

Wednesday 16 September

**Bradford Park Avenue 1 Port Vale 2**

Vale completed their first double of the season when they visited the Park Avenue ground, despite going behind when George Beattie gave the home side the lead after seven minutes. Bob Crosbie squared a quick pass across for Beattie to score with a fine goal. After 14 minutes, Askey forced a corner and when his centre was headed away Mullard hit a first time drive into the top corner. Seven minutes into the second half Vale got the winner when Askey passed to Hayward who swung the ball into a gap for Griffiths to run on and beat Mitch Downie with a clever shot. Reg Potts was injured early in the game but stayed on and played through it, although limping. Dickie Cunliffe helped him out at left back.

46

Vale – King, Turner, Potts, Mullard, Cheadle, Sproson, Askey, Leake, Hayward, Griffiths, Cunliffe
Att 10,960

Roy Sproson said: "Reg Potts had a terribly swollen ankle, which was all the colours of the rainbow. The rest of the lads rallied round to cover him and we managed to win the game."

Saturday 19 September

**Port Vale 2 Workington 0**

Vale took on Workington with the eagerly anticipated derby match against unbeaten Crewe Alexandra to come on the following Monday. Reg Potts missed the game with a knee injury, being replaced by Jim Elsby, Vale's first team change in eight games. It also ended Potts' run of 73 consecutive appearances. In a lacklustre performance, which was put down to the impending derby game, Vale won 2-0 with goals from Albert Leake (27 minutes) and Ken Griffiths (52). Leake's goal was a volley, which gave 'keeper Alan Ford no chance after a knock down by Hayward. The second goal came when a move between Mullard and Hayward resulted in a Griffiths shot, which hit defender George Aitken. The Vale number 10 met the rebound to steer it home at the second attempt.

Vale – King, Turner, Elsby, Mullard, Cheadle, Sproson, Askey, Leake, Hayward, Griffiths, Cunliffe
Att 16,627

Monday 21 September

**Port Vale 1 Crewe Alexandra 0**

The much-awaited derby clash took place with a 5:40pm kick off. Vale were top of the table with only one defeat and Crewe were second and still unbeaten. Potts returned to the team but Derek Tomkinson came in to replace the injured Leake. In a tight game, reflecting the clubs' respective positions, Vale got on top towards the end. After 87 minutes, Roy Sproson checked a Crewe advance, held off two tackles, and weaved his way into a long range shooting position where he hammered a drive too powerful for the diving Peter

Ellison, to send the crowd delirious. The gap at the top of the table was now increased to four points.

Vale – King, Turner, Potts, Mullard, Cheadle, Sproson, Askey, Tomkinson, Hayward, Griffiths, Cunliffe
Att 17,482

There were some complaints about access to the ground amongst the large crowd and the club were considering installing more turnstiles on the Bycars End.

Wednesday 23 September

The Supporters Club presented the club with a cheque for £150. Five Directors were present at the meeting – Chairman F.W. Burgess, W.A. Holdcroft, J.J. Machin, A. McMinn and Alderman G.L. Barber.

Saturday 26 September

**Scunthorpe United 0 Port Vale 2**

Vale were back on their travels the following Saturday when they visited the Old Show Ground to play Scunthorpe United. Albert Leake returned but Potts was again absent through injury, so Elsby once more came into the team. Vale took an early lead after three minutes when Askey cleverly took the ball from Jack Brownsword and passed to Hayward who promptly shot home. Leake got the second goal in the 32nd minute when South African 'keeper Norman Malan ran out of his goal and the Vale striker nipped in to take the ball round the 'keeper and a defender before shooting into an empty net to complete a 2-0 victory.

Vale – King, Turner, Elsby, Mullard, Cheadle, Sproson, Askey, Leake, Hayward, Griffiths, Cunliffe
Att 12,630

Sunday 27 September

Vale fans would be able to celebrate the win at Scunthorpe with an extra sweet cup of tea or maybe even a cake as sugar rationing, which had been in place since January 1940, was brought to an end. But not until tomorrow when the shops opened!

48

Food rationing ended completely in July 1954 when restrictions on the purchase of meat were lifted.

<u>Monday 28 September</u>

**Crewe Alexandra 0 Port Vale 0**

A week after the home game with Crewe Alexandra, Vale travelled to Gresty Road for the return game on Monday 28 September. The match kicked off at 5:10pm and the gate was boosted by the decision of the Crewe Railway Works management to allow workers to finish 55 minutes earlier than usual. There were also dozens of coaches from the Potteries, contributing towards a record attendance of 17,883. The gates were actually closed, leaving many supporters locked outside. In the days that followed Crewe came under fire for not making the game all ticket.

The previous attendance record for Gresty Road was 14,402 for the Cheshire Senior Cup Final between Macclesfield and Northwich in April 1950. Spectators surged in front of the concrete barriers and perched on the framework and roof of the stand on the popular side.

Reg Potts returned but, due to injuries, Vale had three reserves in the team compared to what was now becoming their recognised first eleven – Derek Tomkinson, Roland Lewis and Mick Hulligan came in for Leake, Hayward and Cunliffe, who were all injured in the Scunthorpe game. The game finished 0-0 to preserve Vale's four point lead at the top, with Crewe remaining in second place. Vale had still only conceded 4 goals in their 13 league games to date.

Vale – King, Turner, Potts, Mullard, Cheadle, Sproson, Askey, Tomkinson, Lewis, Griffiths, Hulligan
Att 17,883

The Vale dressing room was a welter of superstitions and tenaciously cherished tradition. Trainer Ken Fish had to put each player's boots under the bench with the toes pointing out and the shinguards between them, wide ends out. On the bench for each player was a towel, then socks, shorts and, on top, shirts. Any deviation from this order was regarded as the worst of bad luck.

When going out onto the field before a match, goalkeeper Ray King was always last but one in the line, centre-forward Basil

Hayward last. Hayward's socks were never folded like the others but knotted together.

In fact, the order that all the players came out before a game was rigidly stuck to and only changed when there were team changes. For the 'regular' eleven they always came out in this order:

Cheadle, Potts, Cunliffe, Griffiths, Leake, Turner, Askey, Mullard, Sproson, King, Hayward

In his right hand jacket pocket, Manager Freddie Steele fondled a small metal ring that came off his son's tent.

Roy Sproson said: "On one away trip we went to see 'Mother Goose' on a Friday night and had a good result the next day. Thereafter, when we were away, we used to try and find a showing of 'Mother Goose'. We must have seen it four times but we always won!"

There were some discussions nationally about how to improve the finances of third division clubs. Proposals had been made in the past for four clubs to go down from Division 2 and two each to be promoted from Division 3(North) and Division 3(South) but they had never gained the 75% majority at the League's annual meeting necessary for the rules to be altered. So it remained that only two clubs were relegated from Division 2 and only the champions of Division 3(N) and Division 3(S) were promoted!

League table:

|              | P  | W | D | L | F  | A  | PTS |
|--------------|----|---|---|---|----|----|-----|
| PORT VALE    | 13 | 9 | 3 | 1 | 21 | 4  | 21  |
| Crewe Alex   | 13 | 5 | 7 | 1 | 17 | 10 | 17  |
| Wrexham      | 13 | 7 | 2 | 4 | 24 | 17 | 16  |
| Bradford City| 13 | 7 | 2 | 4 | 12 | 13 | 16  |
| Barnsley     | 12 | 5 | 5 | 2 | 19 | 12 | 15  |
| Gateshead    | 13 | 5 | 5 | 3 | 18 | 14 | 15  |

50

# October

Saturday 3 October

**Port Vale 5 York City 0**

Vale achieved their biggest win of the season so far, and of course their biggest at Vale Park since it opened in 1950. Basil Hayward scored after 20 minutes, nodding home a Colin Askey centre after the latter had been sent clear by Mullard. Vale went in at half time 1-0 ahead, but they really went to town in the second half. Nine minutes after the interval, Hayward smashed home a left foot drive from a Dickie Cunliffe cross.

Cunliffe scored himself in the 63$^{rd}$ minute with a fierce rising shot after being set up by a Hayward header before setting Ken Griffiths up to hit home a scorcher after 72 minutes. Eleven minutes from time Derek Tomkinson scored his first of the season with a header from a Griffiths cross.

Vale – King, Turner, Elsby, Mullard, Cheadle, Sproson, Askey, Tomkinson, Hayward, Griffiths, Cunliffe
Att: 18,778

Saturday 10 October

**Chesterfield 1 Port Vale 2**

The following Saturday Vale travelled to Saltergate to play Chesterfield, who were unbeaten at home and included Alf Bellis, a former Vale player, in their team. Vale built up a 2-0 half time lead with goals from Ken Griffiths and Colin Askey. After 27 minutes, Griffiths took a pass from Leake and raced through to shoot past the advancing goalkeeper Ronnie Powell. Only five minutes later, Griffiths turned provider when he centred to Askey who shot into the top right-hand corner of the net. Cyril Hatton replied for the home side ten minutes into the second half, shooting home from a Fred Capel free-kick, but Vale held out for another win.

In fact they could have extended their lead three minutes from time when a defender handled a cross from Askey to concede a penalty, but Powell dived to his right to save Albert Mullard's kick. It turned out to be one of only two penalties awarded to Vale in the entire season!

Vale – King, Turner, Elsby, Mullard, Cheadle, Sproson, Askey, Leake, Hayward, Griffiths, Cunliffe
Att: 15,806

On the same day England beat Wales 4-1 at Ninian Park, Cardiff in a World Cup Qualifier in front of a 61,000 crowd.

<u>Monday 12 October</u>

The 1953 Charity Shield took place at Highbury where Arsenal beat Blackpool 3-1. It was the first competitive senior football match in England to be played under floodlights.

**Cheadle, Leake, Askey and Mullard in training**

<u>Friday 16 October</u>

Sir Edmund Hillary, who, along with Tenzing Norgay, had been the first to climb to the summit of Mount Everest the previous May, visited the Victoria Hall, Hanley as part of a lecture tour. The 34-year-old's lecture was a 2,000 sell-out, lasted for 2 hours and included 80 colour transparencies. On reaching the summit of Everest Sir Edmund said that his first feeling was a great sense of relief and his second was a keen desire to go down again as their oxygen was running out!

**Port Vale 2 Tranmere Rovers 0**

Rovers included Cyril Done in their team, who was currently the leading scorer in Division 3(North) with 13 goals to date, and was to join Vale the following season. The Merseysiders also included Harold Bell who hadn't missed a league or cup game since the war! He went on to make a record 401 consecutive league appearances which ended in August 1955. Vale dominated their opponents and, after 24 minutes, Leake shot into the net from close in after bringing the ball under control following a pass by Mullard. Hayward headed home Askey's corner 20 minutes into the second half to complete a 2-0 win.

Vale – King, Turner, Potts, Mullard, Cheadle, Sproson, Askey, Leake, Hayward, Griffiths, Cunliffe
Att: 19,204

Wednesday 21 October

England drew 4-4 with a Rest of the World team at Wembley in a match arranged to commemorate the 90th anniversary of the formation of the FA. Alf Ramsey scored a last minute equaliser for England from the penalty spot.

Saturday 24 October

**Halifax Town 0 Port Vale 1**

Vale's next game was at The Shay, home of Halifax Town, who included Norman Hallam in their team. Hallam had played for Vale during the previous season but was only part-time as he was also a Methodist minister. He had left the Valiants in May 1953 because he had moved house to Doncaster. Vale extended their lead at the top of the table from seven points up to eight with a 1-0 victory courtesy of another goal by Albert Leake, this time from a pass by Dickie Cunliffe. Ken Griffiths also hit the bar twice and the post once!

Vale – King, Turner, Potts, Mullard, Cheadle, Sproson, Askey,
Leake, Hayward, Griffiths, Cunliffe
Att: 10,361

Earlier that day Vale had gone out of the FA Youth Cup in the
first round when they lost 2-1 after extra time at Walsall, in a match
which kicked off at 11am. It was Vale's first ever game in the
competition, not having entered during its inaugural season of
1952/53.

The Sentinel reported that the average gate receipts for reserve
games were £50.

Local cinemas showing films that weekend were the Capitol,
Odeon, Gaumont, Palace and Roxy in Hanley; the Majestic and
Danilo in Stoke; the Rex, Roxy and Savoy in Newcastle-under-Lyme;
the Ritz and Coliseum in Burslem; the Empire in Longton and the
Ritz in Tunstall.

Saturday 31 October

**Port Vale 1 Carlisle United 0**

Vale made it nine wins from their last ten games by defeating
Carlisle United 1-0. There was a taste of autumn rain and mud at
Vale Park with a soft and slippery pitch. Leake again scored with a
tap-in in the 18th minute after Basil Hayward had unselfishly squared
the ball across the goalmouth.
Whenever Tommy Cheadle passed the ball to Albert Leake, or
vice-versa, the supporters used to say it was the longest pass in
football – from Cheadle to Leake (Leek)!

Vale – King, Turner, Potts, Mullard, Cheadle, Sproson, Askey,
Leake, Hayward, Griffiths, Cunliffe
Att: 12,454

Colin Askey said: "Freddie Steele was miles ahead of his time. I
used to watch Stan Matthews and Tom Finney and, when they lost
the ball, they would not bother about getting it back. That was just
what was done then; if you played wide you waited for the service.
Steele made sure we tracked back and used to tell us once we had
lost the ball we were defenders. He'd say that Dickie Cunliffe, the

other winger, and I were fit enough to do our own jobs and get back too. And it worked.

He was very nervous. He hardly ever saw a game finish, preferring to stay in the dressing room with a towel round his head and the taps running to drown out the crowd noise. He used to come in on his push bike with his cycle clips on.

He had an eye for spotting players' best positions and everybody loved him. Everyone was happy and we had a winning mentality. He was rough with you at times but you would still go out and play for him. The lads thought he was funny.

He knew our strengths and weaknesses and those of other teams and he had a simple philosophy. If we had the ball we were attackers, if we did not have the ball we were defenders. It was a team game, none of this standing about. Freddie used to say 'if you want the ball go and bloody get it.' He was also very superstitious and always wore a pair of our black and white socks."

Steele had played as a guest for Arsenal during the Second World War and had studied their methods, basing his defensive style on theirs.

Roy Sproson said: "If we were winning in a tight game, Freddie Steele would disappear for the last 5 minutes and was to be found hiding in the toilet. His superstitions led him to wear a tweed trilby, a pair of black and white hooped football stockings with his suit and let his hair grow long."

Ken Griffiths said: "I never heard anybody talk football like Freddie Steele. I was with him and Bill Shankly for a quarter of an hour and it was Freddie who was doing all the talking. The boss was a great tactician and he told me the system we were playing had been used by Arsenal in 1932."

League table:

|  | P | W | D | L | F | A | PTS |
|---|---|---|---|---|---|---|---|
| PORT VALE | 18 | 14 | 3 | 1 | 32 | 5 | 31 |
| Gateshead | 18 | 9 | 5 | 4 | 28 | 19 | 23 |
| Bradford P A | 17 | 8 | 6 | 3 | 38 | 23 | 22 |
| Crewe Alex | 18 | 7 | 8 | 3 | 22 | 15 | 22 |
| Barnsley | 17 | 7 | 7 | 3 | 26 | 19 | 21 |
| Scunthorpe U | 17 | 7 | 6 | 4 | 29 | 21 | 20 |

# November

Derek Tomkinson played for the Territorial Army in a game against Liverpool on Merseyside.

Saturday 7 November

**Accrington Stanley 2 Port Vale 2**

Vale's next game meant a journey to Peel Park to face Accrington Stanley. It was raining, the pitch was badly churned up and the players were slipping and sliding all over the place on a surface of watery paste. Shortly after Askey had hit the bar, Griffiths sent Cunliffe through and he cut in from the wing to beat Joe Henderson with a low hard shot, the goalkeeper diving and reaching the ball but unable to check its path into goal. That was in the seventh minute and the score remained 1-0 until half-time. After 51 minutes, Hayward sent a pass into the middle from near the corner flag on the left and Griffiths took it forward a pace or two round the 'keeper and scored.

However, Stanley fought back and Ian Brydon reduced the arrears four minutes later. Vale had difficulty clearing the ball in the mud and Bryden nipped in to put the ball in the net. Then the unthinkable happened and Vale conceded a second goal in the same game for the first time that season! Ray King dived full length to push out a brilliant shot from Joe Devlin in the 73rd minute but the ball rolled to Les Cocker who equalised with a low drive, and the game finished 2-2. Cocker went on to find fame and fortune as the coach at Leeds United with Don Revie, and was also the coach of England when they won the World Cup in 1966.

Vale – King, Turner, Potts, Mullard, Cheadle, Sproson, Askey, Leake, Hayward, Griffiths, Cunliffe
Att: 7,895

Monday 9 November

The draw was made for the first round of the FA Cup, and Vale were given a long journey with an away tie at Darlington, where they had already won 3-0 in the league in August.

56

A party of Vale players went to see the England versus Ireland World Cup qualifier at Goodison Park. England won 3-1, with Harold Hassall opening the scoring after 30 seconds.

The 'Panorama' programme began on BBC TV. It is still broadcast today and is the longest running programme on British television.

Saturday 14 November

**Port Vale 2 Grimsby Town 0**

The Mariners proved stubborn opponents but, after 43 minutes, Askey crossed for Leake to head home, with Grimsby's goalkeeper Clarrie Williams reaching the ball but unable to prevent it going in. Twenty minutes into the second half Hayward's shot from Dickie Cunliffe's centre was deflected to Albert Leake who made no mistake in shooting home.
Later in the game Griffiths hit the bar and Hayward the post, but it finished 2-0 which meant that Vale had still only conceded one goal at Vale Park after 10 home games!

Vale – King, Turner, Potts, Mullard, Cheadle, Sproson, Askey, Leake, Hayward, Griffiths, Cunliffe
Att: 14,799

Saturday 21 November

**FA Cup first round:
Darlington 1 Port Vale 3**

Tickets for this FA Cup-tie at Feethams were priced at 9p on the terraces, 18p in the West Stand and an expensive 20p in the East Stand. The referee was Mr H. Webb from Leeds, who had refereed Vale's 5-0 win over York City the previous month and was to play a big part later in Vale's FA cup run. If a replay was to be required it would be at Vale Park on the following Monday afternoon, kick-off 2pm.
Tommy Ward hit the bar for Darlington in the second minute and there was an even more unusual occurrence after 33 minutes when Ray King miskicked a clearance straight to Darlington's Les Robson

who drove the ball straight into the net before anyone could recover. Vale went in 1-0 down at half time, the first time in the season they had gone into the interval behind!

Vale soon rectified matters in the second half as Hayward's 57th minute shot hit the crossbar and Leake scored from the rebound and then, six minutes later, Dickie Cunliffe drove the ball goalwards and Hayward made sure by directing the ball out of the keeper's reach. In the closing minutes of the game Cunliffe clinched Vale's place in round two by scoring their third from Leake's pass.

Vale – King, Turner, Potts, Mullard, Cheadle, Sproson, Askey, Leake, Hayward, Griffiths, Cunliffe
Att: 10,700

Ray King said: "From the moment we played our first league game of the season and beat Mansfield, there was a feeling that something special was going to happen. We had been put out in the early rounds the previous few seasons, but that was history and we already knew we were on a roll when we beat Darlington. However, the game was far from a formality and we only got through after withstanding a barrage from them in the first 20 minutes. But as soon as we scored, we were the team which took control and you could see a surge of confidence shoot through the whole team."

Tuesday 24 November

In the afternoon, the draw for the FA Cup second round was made and Vale were given another away tie, this time at Southport. Ties were to be played on Saturday 12 December at 2:15pm and replays on or before the following Thursday, kick-off 2pm.

Wednesday 25 November

Watched by a party of Vale players and staff, Hungary became the first foreign country to win on English soil as they beat England 6-3 at Wembley. The scoreline could have been even more bizarre as Hungary led 6-3 after 57 minutes!

60 years later the only survivor of that England team is Jackie Sewell, who still watches Notts County, his first club, at the age of 86.

<u>Thursday 26<sup>th</sup> November</u>

The House of Lords voted in favour of the Government's proposal for commercial television. It eventually arrived in the form of ITV in 1955.

<u>Friday 27 November</u>

It was announced that Alan Bennett had been discharged from hospital this week and hoped to start light training in three weeks time.

<u>Saturday 28 November</u>

**Port Vale 6 Rochdale 0**

Vale produced their biggest win of the season so far against their Lancashire opponents. The rout began in the 17<sup>th</sup> minute when Cunliffe centred for Griffiths to neatly pick his way through the Rochdale defence before tapping the ball into the corner of the net. Two minutes later Leake headed home another Cunliffe cross and then, a further ten minutes on, Hayward brought down a cross from Askey for Griffiths to score again. Hayward then hit the post and, after another of the centre-forward's shots had been blocked, Griffiths rammed home the loose ball to complete his hat-trick after 62 minutes.

Vale were rampant and, a minute later, Askey centred for Hayward to score with a header. Ten minutes after that, another Hayward shot was parried by the Dale goalkeeper and Leake drove in the rebound to complete a 6-0 victory and send Vale nine points clear at the top of the table. It was Vale's biggest win since September 1947, when they defeated Watford 7-0.

Vale – King, Turner, Potts, Mullard, Cheadle, Sproson, Askey, Leake, Hayward, Griffiths, Cunliffe
Att: 16,841

**Ken Griffiths completes his hat trick against Rochdale**

A director of another Third Division North club said of the Vale after the game "Is it any use trying to catch them? Without any competition for the leadership hundreds of supporters are beginning to lose interest and it isn't even halfway yet. What's going to happen after Christmas to teams who are out of the cup? Teams can't afford any more losses at the turnstiles." It led to further lobbying for two teams to be promoted instead of one. The Football League was eventually reorganised into Divisions 1, 2, 3 and 4 in 1958, and more teams were promoted.

League table:

|  | P | W | D | L | F | A | PTS |
|---|---|---|---|---|---|---|---|
| PORT VALE | 21 | 16 | 4 | 1 | 42 | 7 | 36 |
| Bradford P A | 20 | 10 | 7 | 3 | 43 | 25 | 27 |
| Gateshead | 21 | 10 | 7 | 4 | 33 | 23 | 27 |
| Scunthorpe U | 20 | 10 | 6 | 4 | 37 | 25 | 26 |
| Barnsley | 20 | 9 | 7 | 4 | 30 | 24 | 25 |
| Stockport Co | 21 | 9 | 6 | 6 | 41 | 27 | 24 |

# December

At the beginning of December it was announced that Hanley shops were to close for Christmas on Friday 25th, Saturday 26th, Sunday 27th (shops were always closed all day on Sundays anyway), and Monday 28th December.

Saturday 5 December

**Wrexham 1 Port Vale 1**

Vale made the short journey to the Racecourse Ground and a white ball was used, which was unusual at the time. Glyn Hughes gave the Welshmen the lead after 20 minutes with a well placed right foot shot and Vale went in behind at half time for the first time that season in a league game. However, Hayward came to Vale's rescue by heading home Askey's cross after 62 minutes. Within a minute Leake fired a shot against the post but that was the end of the scoring in a hard fought draw.

Vale – King, Turner, Potts, Mullard, Cheadle, Sproson, Askey, Leake, Hayward, Griffiths, Cunliffe
Att: 14,570

Friday 11 December

A dramatised feature called 'The Port Vale story – highlights in the history of the Cinderella club of Midland soccer' will be broadcast on BBC radio's Midland Home Service on 6 January 1954.
The script for the programme was written by Barney Bamford. Sir Stanley Rous (Secretary of the FA), Vale Director WA Holdcroft, Freddie Steele and present and former players were to take part.
Two popular actors from the radio soap 'The Archers', Chris Gittins (who played Walter Gabriel in the Archers) and Will Kings (who played Ben White) were to act as storytellers. Recordings for the programme were to be made at Vale Park on 23 December.
The Vale team travelled to Southport the day before the second round FA Cup game and stayed overnight.

A new version of the Vale 'War Cry' was composed for the occasion. As there was a clash of colours, Vale being black and white with Southport usually wearing black and white striped shirts, the rules in the FA Cup at the time were that both teams had to change, with Vale choosing red and white stripes and Southport old gold.

Saturday 12 December

**FA Cup second round:**
**Southport 1 Port Vale 1**

The referee was Mr AW Luty of Leeds which was strange as the referee in Vale's first round win at Darlington was also from Leeds! Mr Luty was later in the season appointed to referee the final.

The game between two teams from Division 3(N) was tight with few chances and Vale looked to have secured their passage into the potentially lucrative third round when Griffiths headed against the upright after 73 minutes and Hayward crashed home a left foot drive from the rebound. However, Southport equalised ten minutes later through a Harry Whitworth header and that was the end of the scoring.

Vale – King, Turner, Potts, Mullard, Cheadle, Sproson, Askey, Leake, Hayward, Griffiths, Cunliffe
Att: 12,529

Ray King said: "We got hammered in the second round at Southport and were fortunate to come away with a draw. I had a stormer in that tie and our manager Freddie Steele said this was my moment. We had a tremendous team spirit, which was what really bonded us together. We never gave up without a fight. Things don't always go your way in games, so you just have to dig in and battle your way through, and that's exactly what happened against Southport."

Ray King was no stranger to Haig Avenue as he had put in some training spells there a few years before with his brother Frank who kept goal for Southport during the war, and was later a Southport fireman and a referee.

Colin Askey said: "To be honest we were lucky to come away from Haig Avenue with the draw."

Roy Sproson said: "We had an awkward match in the second round at Southport where we were outplayed for much of the time. Colin Askey and Albert Leake were limping for three-quarters of the game yet we managed a draw. Team spirit was tremendous."

The replay was scheduled for 2pm the following Monday.
A Sunderland director was in the crowd to watch Stan Turner, but Freddie Steele said that he was not for sale.

Monday 14 December

Should they get through the second round, Vale were drawn away again in the third round against Nuneaton or QPR who had drawn 1-1 at Loftus Road and were to replay at Nuneaton on Thursday. Nuneaton were in the Birmingham Combination League. Third round ties were to be played on Saturday 9 January.

**FA Cup second round replay:**
**Port Vale 2 Southport 0**

Both teams retained their colours from Saturday and Vale were again refereed by an official from Yorkshire. An orange coloured ball was used at the start. Vale took the lead after 18 minutes when Cunliffe flighted the ball into the goalmouth where Hayward headed down and into the net. 18 minutes from the end Vale doubled their lead when Cunliffe's corner was headed across the goal and Askey drove the ball past Wilf Birkett in the Southport goal.

It had been another tough game and Cheadle, Turner, Leake and Griffiths all had various injuries. The actor Terry Thomas was a guest at the game as he was appearing in Hanley and he went into the dressing room afterwards to congratulate the players. Someone else who did likewise was Stanley Matthews, the former Stoke City player, then with Blackpool, the cup holders.

Vale – King, Turner, Potts, Mullard, Cheadle, Sproson, Askey, Leake, Hayward, Griffiths, Cunliffe
Att: 13,024

At a meeting of the Football Association's FA Cup committee it was decided not to vary the kick-off times of FA Cup replays this season, meaning that no floodlighting would be permitted. 14 Football League clubs had floodlights at the time (Vale didn't have any until 1958), an innovation that Freddie Steele was not too keen on. He thought that it would increase the number of games and there would have to be meaningless friendlies to help to pay for them.

Tuesday 15 December

It was announced that, as a result of the joint inquiry conducted by the FA and the Football League into the affairs of Mansfield Town, the Nottinghamshire club has been fined £500 and Freddie Steele, the former Mansfield player-manager, has been fined £250.

The allegations investigated were that illegal payments had been made to Mr Steele and three players – former Welsh international Dai Jones, Johnny Grogan and the ex-Stoke player George Antonio, then the player-manager of Oswestry Town.

The charges were made by the former secretary of Mansfield, WJ Warner. Steele said: "I have been notified of the findings and I have no comment to make." Steele had admitted receiving the payments from WM Hornby (former Chairman of Mansfield). The Commission said that it was satisfied from the evidence that on or about 17 October 1949 and July 1951 WM Hornby had made irregular payments of £50 and £200 to Steele.

FW Burgess, the Vale Chairman said: "Port Vale, although not concerned in any way with this inquiry, are well satisfied with the findings of the Joint Commission. We are glad that Mr Steele's official position with Port Vale is not affected. Port Vale owe him a lot for their present position as Division 3(N) leaders and FA Cup third round challengers.'

WM Hornby, the ex-Chairman of Mansfield, was suspended permanently from football and football management.

Mr EM Smith (former vice-chairman) and Jones were suspended sine die – i.e. until further notice. JA Taylor (Director) was suspended until the end of February 1954. 4 Directors and 1 former Director were cautioned. Grogan was severely censured and Antonio was fined £50.

The Commission had met at Nottingham the previous Thursday.

Thursday 17 December

Vale's Christmas fixtures with Chester were at home on Christmas Day at 11am and away on Boxing Day at 2:30pm. The away game was all-ticket, prices 9p standing and 15p seats.

FW Burgess (Chairman), Freddie Steele, Tommy Cheadle (captain) and Reg Potts (vice captain) went to Nuneaton to watch their FA Cup second round replay against QPR, the winners of which would be at home to Vale in the third round. QPR won 2-1.

<u>Saturday 19 December</u>

**Barnsley 0 Port Vale 1**

Barnsley were 5th in the table and unbeaten at home and they were also the only team so far this season to have earned a point at Vale Park.

After 10 successive games unchanged, Vale were forced into a change when Griffiths failed a fitness test and Tomkinson replaced him. Barnsley were on top in the first half but couldn't find a breakthrough. In the second period Vale pressed forward more and Hayward scored eight minutes after the break with a 25 yard shot. Vale could have scored a second goal on several occasions but had to be satisfied with a single goal victory.

Vale – King, Turner, Potts, Mullard, Cheadle, Sproson, Askey, Leake, Hayward, Tomkinson, Cunliffe
Att: 11,426

<u>Wednesday 23 December</u>

Ken Higgs, a 16 year old Port Vale centre-half, was selected to play in a trial game for the FA Youth XI against the Manchester Youth XI in Manchester on 9 January.

<u>Friday 25 December</u>

**Port Vale 1 Chester 0**

Supporters couldn't linger too much over opening their Christmas presents as this match kicked off at 11am! It turned out to be Vale's last ever Christmas Day home game. Ken Griffiths returned to the team in place of Tomkinson and Basil Hayward scored the only goal with a rocket shot in the 72nd minute to extend Vale's unbeaten run to 19 games. Tommy Cheadle pulled a muscle in the first ten minutes of the game.

Vale – King, Turner, Potts, Mullard, Cheadle, Sproson, Askey, Leake, Hayward, Griffiths, Cunliffe
Att: 15,322

Saturday 26 December

**Chester 0 Port Vale 1**

As was the practice in those days, teams played the same opposition in both holiday games. Special trains took Vale fans to Chester for 28p departing from the following stations: Tunstall, Burslem, Cobridge, Hanley, Longton, Stoke, Blythe Bridge, Meir, Normacot, Fenton, Etruria, Longport, Kidsgrove and Alsager.
Vale completed a quick double over their Cheshire rivals when Hayward headed home from a Griffiths cross on 69 minutes. It was the eighth successive game in which he had scored, a club record that still stands today. Cheadle ended a run of 74 consecutive appearances after straining a leg muscle in the Christmas Day game. Tomkinson was the replacement and some positional changes were made. Reg Potts deputised as captain.

Vale – King, Turner, Potts, Mullard, Sproson, Leake, Askey, Tomkinson, Hayward, Griffiths, Cunliffe
Att: 10,979

Thursday 31 December

Tickets for the FA Cup third round tie at QPR went on sale at 23p and 30p. Special train tickets to London Euston were also on sale at £1.23.

League table:

|  | P | W | D | L | F | A | PTS |
|---|---|---|---|---|---|---|---|
| PORT VALE | 25 | 19 | 5 | 1 | 46 | 8 | 43 |
| Gateshead | 26 | 13 | 8 | 5 | 44 | 27 | 34 |
| Barnsley | 24 | 12 | 7 | 5 | 35 | 26 | 31 |
| Stockport Co | 25 | 11 | 7 | 7 | 53 | 33 | 29 |
| Bradford P A | 24 | 10 | 9 | 5 | 45 | 31 | 29 |
| Scunthorpe U | 24 | 11 | 7 | 6 | 41 | 35 | 29 |

66

# January

<u>Saturday 2<sup>nd</sup> January</u>

Fog blanketed the country and the Vale's scheduled home game with Darlington was called off for that reason by referee Mr E. Crawford at 2.10 pm. The turnstiles hadn't been opened for the game, due to kick off at 2.30, because of the doubt and the news was relayed over loudspeakers to the thousands waiting outside.

Opponents Darlington had played a home game the day before and travelled immediately afterwards, staying overnight in Macclesfield. Tommy Cheadle was particularly disappointed, as he had recovered from injury. The good news for Vale was that their nearest challengers in the league, Gateshead, lost 5-0 at struggling Chester.

Roland Lewis, whom Vale had released on a free transfer in December, joined Witton Albion.

<u>Wednesday 6<sup>th</sup> January</u>

The Port Vale story was broadcast on Midlands Regional radio. The 20 minute feature, written by Barney Bamford of Penkhull, was recorded before Christmas.

The club received planning permission to build the Railway Stand, costing £25,000. The directors said that they didn't know how they were going to pay for it, but were going ahead anyway as an act of faith!

<u>Saturday 9<sup>th</sup> January</u>

**FA Cup third round**
**QPR 0 Port Vale 1**

Instead of a league game at home to Bradford City, Vale triumphed away to Third Division (South) opposition to progress into the last 32 of the FA Cup with a hard fought victory. Vale played in their change strip of red and white striped shirts and black shorts in a game that was played in pouring rain. The pitch was very muddy, even waterlogged in parts, and some of it bordered on the farcical at times.

Colin Askey and Dickie Cunliffe were a threat early on, and Ken Griffiths broke clear of the defence only for Guy Taylor to make a last minute tackle.

Vale scored the only goal of the game in the 50th minute. Cunliffe played a long ball from the left, which Albert Leake controlled in fine style, before firing past Harry Brown in the Rangers goal. Brian Nicholas had a chance to equalise, but generally Vale remained in charge. Basil Hayward had a shot blocked with Cunliffe firing the rebound over the bar and then Leake hit the post as Vale threatened to extend their lead. Tommy Cheadle picked up another knock.

As the game wore on some of the players could hardly walk in the mud, and virtually all of the pitch markings had disappeared.

Vale – King, Turner, Potts, Mullard, Cheadle, Sproson, Askey, Leake, Hayward, Griffiths, Cunliffe
Att: 17,474

Ray King said: "They always said Division Three South was more skilful than Division Three North but we put them right on that score. Albert Leake got the only goal. He was our goal-getter on the Cup run, while I tried to keep things shored up at the back behind our 'Iron Curtain.'"

An incredible 15 of the 32 ties ended in draws and so would require replays. Grimsby drew 5-5 with Fulham and five of the other games finished 3-3!

Many of the Vale fans had travelled by special train, which didn't actually begin the return journey until 9.45 pm so that the fans could celebrate in London afterwards, something that was always planned irrespective of the score!

## Monday 11th January

The draw for the 4th Round of the FA Cup gave Vale a tough looking away tie at First Division Cardiff City.

Alan Bennett was discharged from the army, having recovered from illness. Roy Brien was also about to be released from the forces, with illness delaying matters.

**Hartlepools United 2 Port Vale 1**

Derek Tomkinson came in for the injured Tommy Cheadle, as the defence was re-shuffled.

The game began in a gale storm and soon after the start the crowd were treated to the sight of Freddie Steele's hat being blown off which resulted in him haring down the touchline after it! A clearance from a defender also got caught by the wind and blew out of the ground.

Vale took the lead in the 26<sup>th</sup> minute. Dickie Cunliffe did well on the left surging past Joe Willetts, and his cross into the middle was nodded on by Basil Hayward for Ken Griffiths to sweep home. Soon afterwards home defender Wattie Moore almost scored an own goal with a header but 'keeper Berry Brown just about saved it. Moore went on to make more league appearances than any other player for 'Pool, 447 by the time he retired in 1964.

Hartlepools drew level in the 34<sup>th</sup> minute. Fred Richardson took a throw in to Tommy McGuigan and he fired the ball into the bottom corner of the net. At half time there was a fire under the press box and the fire brigade were called to deal with the situation, which was soon under control and no-one was hurt.

Hayward headed wide as Vale moved forward but then Hartlepools went in front on the hour mark. Eric Wildon did well on the left before playing the ball in to McGuigan and he made no mistake with a low shot.

Ray King injured his knee in a goalmouth scramble and couldn't take goal kicks for the next few games or do any training.

Hartlepools were certainly a bogey side having also been the only visiting team to score at Vale Park so far! The defeat brought to an end Vale's undefeated run of 21 games, a record which still stands today.

Vale – King, Turner, Potts, Mullard, Sproson, Leake, Askey, Tomkinson, Hayward, Griffiths, Cunliffe
Att: 8,554

Monday 18<sup>th</sup> January

More hardcore was needed to build the foundations for the new Railway Stand and the club put out an appeal for anyone who wished to donate some – for free.

**Port Vale 0 Gateshead 0**

Tommy Cheadle was fit to return with Derek Tomkinson being the one to drop out for a game between the top two in the league, which attracted the biggest crowd of the season thus far.

Vale began the game well and Cunliffe fired over the bar. It was Gateshead who came closest to taking the lead though when John Ingham hit the post in the 23rd minute with Roy Sproson hacking the rebound to safety. Basil Hayward went on a mazy run that ended with a shot saved by Bob Gray in the visitor's goal.

Colin Askey and Hayward both had headers saved and the Vale did get the ball in the net after a scramble, only for it to be disallowed. In the 77th minute Hayward nodded an Askey cross down to Ken Griffiths but he only succeeded in knocking the ball wide.

The game ended Vale's 12 game run of consecutive home wins, still a club record 60 years later. Gateshead became the first team to take three points off the Vale that season.

Vale – King, Turner, Potts, Mullard, Cheadle, Sproson, Askey, Leake, Hayward, Griffiths, Cunliffe
Att: 20,370

Thursday 28 January

Ken Higgs, a member of the Port Vale ground staff, who had just celebrated his 17th birthday and lived in Sandyford, was selected to play for England against Scotland in a Youth international at Middlesbrough on Saturday 6 February. Higgs also played cricket for Meakins in the North Staffs League as an opening batsman and bowler and was later to play Test Cricket for England.

At a meeting of the Port Vale Supporters Club (Northern Area) Chairman FW Burgess suggested that the bulk of the £25,000 needed for a new stand at Vale Park could be raised by regular supporters taking out season tickets. He said he was getting tired of 'passing the hat round' and appealed to supporters to take out season tickets in advance for next season.

Director Joe Machin said the new ground had already cost £95,000 and loans had had to be taken up. He said a match attendance of 19,000, which brought in about £1,900, was reduced to £1,100 when entertainment tax and payment for visitors had been paid. The one hundred club, in which people paid £100 to sit in the directors box all season had 21 vacancies. The wages bill was £450 per week.

Reports from Cardiff, where Vale were due to play their fourth round FA Cup tie on Saturday, said the pitch was covered in snow.

Friday 29 January

The Vale party left by train in the morning and were invited to tour a Cardiff biscuit factory in the afternoon! After dinner, the players were entertained at an evening theatre show. The party were to return on Saturday evening in a special compartment attached to one of the supporters' trains.

Vale were at full strength with Derek Tomkinson and Jim Elsby travelling as reserves. Ray King had constant treatment all day for the bad knee he had injured at Hartlepools though.
The weather was freezing, with frost day and night. The temperature the previous night was 16F (-9C) and Thursday had been the coldest day since 1947. Snow fell heavily in Cardiff and the Ninian Park pitch was covered to a depth of 3 inches (7.6 cm). The under surface was very hard. A Scottish well wisher had sent the Vale a consignment of white heather for good luck!

If a replay was necessary it would take place at Vale Park the following Thursday afternoon. This was decided by the FA after Vale and Cardiff had failed to fix a date by mutual agreement. Vale would have preferred a Monday replay as was their custom and because they were committed to the long journey to Workington on the Friday for the following Saturday's league match.

Saturday 30 January

**FA Cup fourth Round**
**Cardiff City 0 Port Vale 2**

Vale faced their toughest task of the season thus far with a trip to first division Cardiff City, but were backed by a large contingent of fans despite the snowy conditions. Ray King passed a fitness test to the relief of everyone connected with the Vale and Stan Turner also played despite suffering from a sore throat. The pitch was rock hard but flat.

In the early stages Vale advanced and had two corners in succession, but from the second one Cardiff goalkeeper Ron Howells collided with defender Derek Sullivan and was knocked unconscious. He was carried off on a stretcher and taken to hospital in the 20th minute, and with no substitutes allowed in those days Welsh international defender Alf Sherwood took over the gloves.

Vale then sensed that they could pull off a shock and attacked the ten men and went close on a number of occasions. On the half-hour mark they won a corner and as Basil Hayward headed the ball goalwards, Charlie Rutter just managed to nod the ball off the line. In the 38th minute though, Vale took the lead. Colin Askey, a constant thorn in Cardiff's flesh, advanced down the right and delivered a cross which Hayward squared to Albert Leake, and he picked his spot to score with a low drive.

At half time it was revealed that Howells had regained consciousness in hospital. Vale increased their lead within 30 seconds of the second half getting underway. Albert Mullard easily beat Sullivan, the stand-in left back, and from his centre Ken Griffiths gleefully drove the ball home.

The conditions had prompted Freddie Steele to tell the players to use Askey and Cunliffe on the wings as often as they could and they responded brilliantly, carrying the instructions out to the letter. It was Vale who threatened further goals and Cunliffe and Mullard both went close to scoring. Cardiff's much-vaunted striker Trevor Ford was kept in check by Tommy Cheadle although both had bruises to show for their efforts. At the time Ford had cost more in transfer fees than any other British player, £69,000 from three moves.

Near the end there was a flare up between George Edwards and Stan Turner, and when the referee spoke to Edwards some Cardiff fans threw snowballs at him and the linesman! He later said that at least it warmed him up a bit but that he would still report it to the FA. After the game a crowd gathered at the players entrance and the police had to be called to break it up.

Vale – King, Turner, Potts, Mullard, Cheadle, Sproson, Askey, Leake, Hayward, Griffiths, Cunliffe
Att 27,295

Ray King said: "They had a fearsome centre-forward called Trevor Ford, who I used to have some right battles with. In those days, goalkeepers weren't overprotected like they are these days.

One time, I went up for a high ball and he just followed straight through on me. So, the next time, I returned the favour and he just grunted.

There were always forwards who would go for you. I remember once hearing two say 'Come on, let's get Kingy.' They did, but I survived all right, and we got through this game despite a bit of the rough stuff."

Roy Sproson said, "We had many stirring FA Cup encounters on the FA Cup run in 1953/54. I remember going to Cardiff, then of the First Division, for a match that was doubtful because of the conditions. All the lads were nervous and conflicting reports reached us while we were in the snooker room at our hotel on the morning of the game. We sighed with relief when wrongly told the match was off; then fear returned when it was actually on. The pitch was hard and icy, eventually declared fit and we won 2-0 in a tremendous battle.

I will always remember the duel between Tommy Cheadle and Cardiff's Trevor Ford. Pound for pound they were probably the two hardest men I have known, yet they came off with a smile and handshake at the finish, battered and bruised having gone at each other hammer and tongs for 90 minutes! Then there was the reception afterwards when we reached Cardiff station. It was a sea of Vale faces, an incredible sight."

On the way home, one of the supporters' trains fell foul of the wintry conditions. Fan Jack Millward: "The train got stuck in a snowdrift just before it got to Hereford. The passengers had to get out, scoop the snow off the track and push the train up a hill! The train arrived back 8 hours late."

League table:

|  | P | W | D | L | F | A | PTS |
|---|---|---|---|---|---|---|---|
| PORT VALE | 27 | 19 | 6 | 2 | 47 | 10 | 44 |
| Gateshead | 31 | 15 | 10 | 6 | 52 | 34 | 40 |
| Barnsley | 29 | 15 | 8 | 6 | 49 | 35 | 38 |
| Bradford City | 29 | 15 | 4 | 10 | 43 | 36 | 34 |
| Scunthorpe U | 28 | 12 | 9 | 7 | 43 | 38 | 33 |
| Southport | 29 | 12 | 8 | 9 | 45 | 39 | 32 |

# February

The FA Cup fifth round draw was made and, for the first time in the 1953/54 season, Vale were drawn at home. Their opponents would be the FA Cup holders Blackpool or West Ham, who would be replaying on Wednesday after a 1-1 draw at Upton Park on Saturday. It was the first time since 1928 that Vale had reached the fifth round.

Before the fourth round FA Cup tie against Vale, Cardiff had offered £25,000 for Colin Askey. The offer coincided with Vale's announcement that a time limit had been set for the erection of their new £25,000 stand, but it was firmly turned down. After the match Cardiff offered a 'blank cheque' but Vale replied 'Askey stays with us and we will find the money for the stand another way'.

Colin Askey said: "It was a freezing day in Cardiff, but I had done well and we had won. After the game they had put in an offer for me of £25,000. The offer was turned down.
I remember going in to training on the Monday after the game. I was a bit late and was walking down the terrace towards the rest of the lads when they started to clap me. I thought it was strange but apparently it was because a team like Cardiff had made that sort of an offer for me. That was something special.
When the offer was turned down, Cardiff told Vale to name their price. I didn't know anything about that at the time. I was kept in the dark. I found out eventually by reading the Sentinel some time later."

At various times, Chelsea, Manchester City, Liverpool and West Brom all inquired about Colin Askey.

Tuesday 2 February

The press made a big story about Vale's win at Cardiff, and the club said that one of the main reasons that they won was because they all had a pre-match steak meal at 'The Garrick' in Hereford. This story apparently inspired Aldo and Frank Berni to consider opening a steak house. The Italian brothers who lived in Wales opened their first Berni Inn in Bristol in 1955 and ended up with 147 by the time they sold them in 1970!

## Wednesday 3 February

Cup holders Blackpool beat West Ham 3-1 in their fourth round replay to set up a fifth round tie at Vale Park. A party from the Vale playing staff watched the game.

By coincidence, Freddie Steele was manager of Mansfield Town when their fine FA Cup run of 1950/51 ended in a 2-0 defeat against Blackpool at Bloomfield Road in the fifth round.

The main draw in the Blackpool side was the 38-year-old Hanley born winger Stanley Matthews, who was a Vale supporter in his youth. He went on to sign for Stoke City though, moving to Blackpool in 1947 and famously helping them to win the FA Cup in 1953, in what became known as 'The Matthews Final'.

## Thursday 4 February

It was announced that the Vale vs Blackpool fifth round FA Cup tie on 20 February would be all ticket with a crowd limit of 42,000. This was decided following a conference between the Vale Directors and the Chief Constable of Stoke-on-Trent, Mr FL Bunn, at Vale Park. Admission prices were set at: Seating 40p, Standing 20p on the Railway and Lorne Street sides of the ground, and 13p behind the goals at the Bycars and Hamil Road ends. After inspecting the stadium the Chief Constable said "We have set a limit of 42,000 subject to precautionary measures being taken, such as levelling parts of the terraces and the erection of further barriers and fences". In those days it was mandatory to allow the away team to have 25% of the capacity should they require it and Blackpool indicated that they would require their full quota of the tickets, 10,500.

Vale season ticket holders were requested to submit their claims for 40p seats by Saturday 13 February. For other supporters, tickets were to be sold at the Cheshire League home match with Winsford United on the coming Saturday, when the gates would be opened at 1:30pm. Unsold tickets were then to be put on sale from the following Monday.

## Friday 5 February

Vale were due to travel to Workington, who were on a good run with only two defeats in their last 14 games. Alan Bennett was fit to return to the reserve team after a long absence due mainly to illness, having had to enter hospital due to an 'internal complaint'.

Vale declined with thanks an offer from Stoke to loan them the Victoria Ground for the Blackpool cup tie. Instead, Vale continued printing tickets ready to go on sale the following day; there were different colours to designate which part of the ground the ticket was for: Lorne Street – white and blue, Bycars – salmon, Hamil Road – yellow, and Railway – green.

Prices were also announced for season tickets for the new 4,850 seater Railway Stand which it was announced would be ready for the opening game of the following season: £6.30 for the centre block and £5.25 for the wings.

Saturday 6 February

Queuing for tickets for the cup tie started at 9:30, four hours before the gates opened for the reserve match with Winsford United. The first arrival was a Mr B Butler of 13, Clive Street, Tunstall. Well into the afternoon the PMT bus company ran a two-way service of special buses to and from Vale Park. By 1:15 pm a queue at the 20p turnstile snaked for 100 yards, three and four deep, out into Hamil Road, and crowds were still rolling up. Each spectator would only be allowed one ticket for the cup tie. Tickets were still being sold when the reserve match kicked off. About 6,000 stayed to watch the reserve game, the most for any Cheshire League game that season up to that point. Vale reserves lost 3-2 to Winsford, with Patrick Willdigg and Len Barber scoring for the home side.

Blackpool were likely to bring the FA Cup with them to the match for display. But for a long absence due to injury Eric Hayward, born in Wolstanton and formerly with Vale from 1934 to 1937, might have been in the Blackpool team at centre-half to oppose his brother Basil, the Vale centre-forward! Eric had previously played for Blackpool in the 1948 and 1951 FA Cup Finals.

President Tom Flint was previously a footballer and a referee; also a cricketer and crown green bowler. He had also been a City Councillor. In 1954 he was continuing to follow the Vale from his sick room due to ill health.

**Workington 2 Port Vale 0**

Some of the Vale forwards tried new, rubber soled, boots provided especially in case the ground was frozen. If they had proved a success, they would have been used as a stand by for the cup tie. A Blackpool director took a scouting party up to Borough Park to see the match. Workington's new manager was Bill Shankly, appointed the previous month. He went on to manage Liverpool in 1959 when they were in Division 2 and became one of the most famous British managers of all time, leading them to the Second Division Championship before then going on to win three First Division Championships, two FA Cups, four Charity Shields and a UEFA Cup.

Workington took the lead after half an hour, Norman Mitchell driving the ball low into the net giving Ray King little chance. Eight minutes into the second half, Joe Johnson crossed for Hugh Cameron to head into the net for the home side's second goal. The referee consulted the linesman as he thought the ball might have gone out of play before it was crossed, but he gave the goal.

It turned out to be the Vale's heaviest defeat of the season.

Vale – King, Turner, Potts, Mullard, Cheadle, Sproson, Askey, Leake, Hayward, Griffiths, Cunliffe
Att: 13,714

Ray King said, " My father was living in the north east and only went to three games that season, Gateshead, Hartlepools and Workington. They were the only league games that we lost all season!"

Monday 8 February

Heavy snowfall greeted the start of the new working week, around 18 inches (46 cm) around Vale Park but drifts of up to 7 feet (over 2 metres) were reported on the moors beyond Leek.

A 'No tickets on sale' notice was put up outside the Vale offices but a large crowd had gathered hoping some were left over from Saturday. Statements from the Directors and the Police were necessary before the supporters would disperse.

Tuesday 9 February

The film 'From Here to Eternity' starring Burt Lancaster, Frank Sinatra and Deborah Kerr was showing at the Odeon cinema in

Hanley. The movie went on to win the Oscar for Best Picture at the Academy Awards the following month.

**Vale players have a practice game in the snow**

Despite the previous day's announcement of the Blackpool match being a sell-out, fans were still besieging Vale Park by phone, post and personal call in the hope of getting a ticket. Chairman FW Burgess said "Having done our best we can only be very sorry indeed for those who have been unlucky. We are being hopelessly pressed on all sides for tickets". Supporters Club members were guaranteed tickets. The gate receipts were expected to be more than £7,000 gross; a third of the net receipts would go to the FA and another third to the visiting team.

Wednesday 10 February

More crush barriers were erected at Vale Park in readiness for the cup tie.

Friday 12 February

It was announced by a Ministry of Health Advisory Committee that there is a relation between smoking and lung cancer.

Saturday 13 February

An additional press box was being erected at Vale Park as most newspapers and agencies in the country were to be represented at the cup tie, including newsreel cameramen.

**Port Vale 0 Scunthorpe United 0**

The Vale Park pitch was sticky and muddy after the snow had been cleared. Vale were on top for long periods of this game but couldn't find a breakthrough. Basil Hayward had a shot, which hit the Scunthorpe goalkeeper Norman Malan under the chin, and the custodian had to receive attention for an injured jaw bone! In the first minute of the second half Sproson crashed in a shot which hit the upright. There were several near misses from Hayward, Leake and Griffiths, and towards the end Mullard hit the bar but the game remained goalless. Joe Smith, the Blackpool manager, was at the game.

Jack Brownsword, who went on to make a record 595 league appearances for 'the Iron', was in the Scunthorpe team. In recognition of his long service, the road leading to their current ground Glanford Park, is called Jack Brownsword Way.

Vale – King, Turner, Potts, Mullard, Cheadle, Sproson, Askey, Leake, Hayward, Griffiths, Cunliffe
Att: 17,240

Tuesday 16 February

During training, Freddie Steele asked Colin Askey to impersonate Stanley Matthews in a series of practices so that Reg Potts and Roy Sproson could practice their routine for stopping the Blackpool winger.

Such was the pressure on the staff that Vale used the services of team captain Tommy Cheadle and some of the young players to help cope with the heavy mail and office work.

Almost 100 police were earmarked for duty inside and outside the ground on Saturday.

The Blackpool team were to leave on Friday morning and all but one of them would stay at the Castle Hotel in Newcastle-under-Lyme on Friday night. The exception was Stanley Matthews who, along with his family, would stay with his mother at 63, Seymour Street, Hanley.

**The Castle Hotel, Newcastle-under-Lyme**

Thursday 18 February

A 75 year old from 32 Hardingswood Road, Kidsgrove, John Capper, received some publicity in that he was going to the Blackpool game although almost blind. He went to nearly all the home games at the time on the Hamil End with his wife and she gave him a running commentary.

He used to live in Ricardo Street, Middleport (since renamed Ellers Grove) and professed to having seen the Vale play on all 6 of their home grounds at Limekiln Lane Longport, Westport, Moorland Road Burslem, Athletic Ground Cobridge, Recreation Ground Hanley and Vale Park. Mr Capper said that the name of the club came from the trade name on the brick of a firm of brick manufacturers in Middleport. While he was working at AJ Wilkinson's pottery some years previously, Mr Capper found a brick under a boiler bed and said 'They reckoned then that it was fifty years old. On the front were the words 'H Jones and Company Limited' and on the back 'Burslem Port Vale''.

Mr Capper said that he made enquiries and discovered that there was a firm of that name in Middleport at one time but that it was demolished long ago. Burslem Port Vale was indeed the trade name on their bricks, he was told, and lads working at the firm used to play football on Saturday afternoons on a pitch near the bottom of Porthill Bank. They appropriately called themselves Burslem Port Vale, apparently after the brick name.

He asserted that the first Port Vale team had its origins there and later moved over to its first headquarters in Middleport. Port Vale House was only a few hundred yards from the spot where the brickworks were built.

Mr Capper said that his greatest dream was of Port Vale playing West Bromwich Albion, at the time one of the country's top teams, in the FA Cup Final at Wembley.

Thousands of tons of ashes, including hard core and pit shale, were used to solidify and extend the embankments at Vale Park and 40 additional crush barriers had been erected. Fifteen lorries had been continually in use and on average 30 workmen a day had been engaged.

Saturday 20 February

Blackpool had seven full internationals in their team – Matthews, Johnston, Taylor and Shimwell (England) and Farm, Brown and Kelly (Scotland).

Joe Smith, the Blackpool manager, had spent his childhood in North Staffordshire. He was brought to Newcastle-under-Lyme as a baby by his parents from Dudley Port where he was born in 1889, and stayed until he began his football career with Bolton Wanderers. He attended Ryecroft School and then went to work with his father at Knutton forge. As a youthful footballer he played for Newcastle PSA and won a Sentinel Cup medal when they beat North Stafford Nomads in 1908. The following day he signed for Bolton Wanderers! Joe said "Bolton knocked me up at 6am and I went to the 'Bird in Hand' in Newcastle where I signed for £2.50 per week." While with Bolton Wanderers as a player, he was in their FA Cup winning team twice, in 1923 in the famous White Horse final, the first at Wembley Stadium and 1926. He also played 5 full internationals for England.

The sun was shining but the pitch was heavy after Friday's rain. Stanley Matthews strolled alone into Vale Park at 10:15 and commented, looking at the sun, "It's a pity this weather didn't arrive earlier". Fans started queuing at the turnstiles at 11am and the gates were due to open at 1pm. Ken Fish, the Vale trainer, was celebrating his 40th birthday that very day!

The Hamil Road approach to Vale Park took on the appearance of an open air market. Sellers of favours, rattles, fruits, sweets, souvenirs and Blackpool rock took up positions along the route as the crowds grew. Blackpool fans were offering 13p ground tickets for sale for as much as £1 but trade was not very brisk due to rumours of a number of forged tickets. Plans were made to broadcast a running commentary of the game to crowds outside the ground. It was Blackpool's biggest football exodus since the previous year's cup final. It was like a Bank Holiday in reverse, with Blackpool coming to Stoke-on-Trent! There were seven special trains and over 150 coaches. Because of fowl pest restrictions, Blackpool had not brought their famous live duck mascot.

Spectators included George Formby, who sat with Mr Ellis Smith, MP for Stoke-on-Trent South, Tom Barker and Alderman and Mrs JH Dale. According to one of the Vale players, Stanley Matthews was supposed to get tickets for Formby and asked Freddie Steele for some. Even though he had some in his pocket, he told Stan that he had none! When the player asked why he did that Steele said, "Matthews is a worrier, so why not make him worry a bit more?" Formby did get tickets from elsewhere.

The cup-tie fever, which gripped the whole district, had its repercussions in Newcastle-under-Lyme where hundreds of people gathered outside the Castle Hotel for a glimpse of the Blackpool team. So great was the throng that a police escort had to be provided for the players' coach.

Stoke City's home game with Plymouth Argyle was postponed because of the cup-tie.

Perched high on top of a 40 feet wall, overlooking the Lorne Street turnstiles, schoolchildren had seized the opportunity for a free look at the game.

82

Inside the ground before the kick-off the tightly packed crowd were kept amused by the antics of mascots and comic figures ranged along the touchline, ranging from Charlie Chaplin to Mae West. A Vale fan, in flowing white silk shirt, top hat and black shorts, got the crowd laughing by dribbling a rubber ball up and down. Many of the Vale fans wore black and white top hats and the Vale cheerleader Stephen Dawson also carried a black and white umbrella. Stephen's son Denis later became the club groundsman for many years.

**Blackpool fans before the game**

According to Colin Askey: "Our whole team had been to Wembley the year before to watch the FA Cup Final when Blackpool beat Bolton 4-3 and it was almost unbelievable that we were going to be on the same pitch as Blackpool. I had grown up watching Stan Matthews from the terraces and was his biggest fan. I idolised the bloke; he was like a god to me."

On the morning of the game the middle of the pitch was that wet groundsman Len Parton found it impossible to roll it. What he did do was to drag a heavy plank with rope attached to either end to sweep off any excess water! Len remained the Vale groundsman until moving to Stoke City in 1966.

**Tommy Cheadle leads out the Vale against Blackpool, followed as usual by Reg Potts**

Roy Sproson said: "Before the game Freddie Steele sat with each lad and had a quiet word in his ear. In the meantime, Blackpool were out on the pitch, freezing, kicking heavy practice balls, which Fred had had soaked in water. He kept the Vale players in the dressing room until eventually the referee had to bang on the door for us to come out. The referee almost broke the door down but Fred would have none of it. We did not take to the field until the referee was in the centre circle, so there was no time for a kick about. We were like greyhounds in a trap; when the whistle went we tore into them."

**FA Cup fifth round:**
**Port Vale 2 Blackpool 0**

The pitch was in far better condition than had been expected. Sacks, which had been used to soak up much of the water in the middle, had been removed and the ground had been rolled and sanded. Vale kicked off towards the Hamil End, facing the sun, and were first to show when Hayward headed just wide from Askey's corner kick. After 14 minutes, Cunliffe had a shot which was deflected for a corner. The Vale left winger took the corner himself and Leake rose to head a glorious goal.

**Albert Leake's first goal**

Following this, Vale had had two more corners, which were scrambled away by the beleaguered Blackpool defence, but this was a prelude to Vale doubling their lead. Hayward sent a low pass into the Blackpool goalmouth where Leake raced in to shoot it into the net. There were near misses at both ends and both goalkeepers were in action.

In the 50<sup>th</sup> minute, Griffiths ran onto a through ball from Askey and shot past Farm but the ball hit the foot of an upright and rebounded back into play.

When Blackpool did attack, the home defence showed its true worth and every man pulled his weight. It was rousing stuff to make the blood tingle, and try as they did Blackpool could not penetrate this defence in depth, and Vale's advances still carried the greater danger.

**Blackpool's goalkeeper George Farm beats Albert Leake to the ball – in the background is the Railway Paddock**

As the last minutes ticked away the crowd began to set up a great roar and policemen came out to line the running track. At the finish Vale were still pressing, although Mullard injured his right knee and was limping on the touchline with a blanket round his shoulder. Then the final whistle blew and there were scenes of great joy, with spectators swarming onto the pitch.

Although hard-fought, the game had been remarkably clean with Vale conceding only seven free-kicks and Blackpool just three. The corner count was even with both teams having five.

Vale – King, Turner, Potts, Mullard, Cheadle, Sproson, Askey, Leake, Hayward, Griffiths, Cunliffe
Att: 42,000

**Ken Griffiths beats Farm with a terrific shot, but sees the ball hit a post**

Colin Askey: "Our pitch was heavy and Freddie Steele had a plan. He had played with Stanley Matthews at Stoke and knew him inside out. He wanted to force him inside on to his left foot and where there would be less room to hurt us.

Dickie Cunliffe and Roy Sproson did a fantastic job in blocking off the line and, combined with the state of the pitch, Stan just couldn't cope. It was the worst game I'd ever seen him have.

We were a good team, but we were brilliant that day. I had a good day. I turned it on a bit and thoroughly enjoyed it. In those days there were still very few cars around, so I had ordered a taxi to get home. I had to walk along Park Road in Burslem and the Blackpool fans were getting on buses. They applauded me as I walked along the road. It was a lovely feeling."

Ray King said: "This was fantastic; you never forget when you're involved in a beautiful game like this. Blackpool were the Cup holders after the famous Matthews final the year before, but we were on top form and put them out. Stan came up to me after the game and he was flaked out because he had wanted to do so well and had covered every blade of grass on that pitch for his team's cause. In those days, we had a reputation for being a very defensive side but that wasn't the case. We used to play it out from the back and the way we played that day proved we were definitely a footballing side."

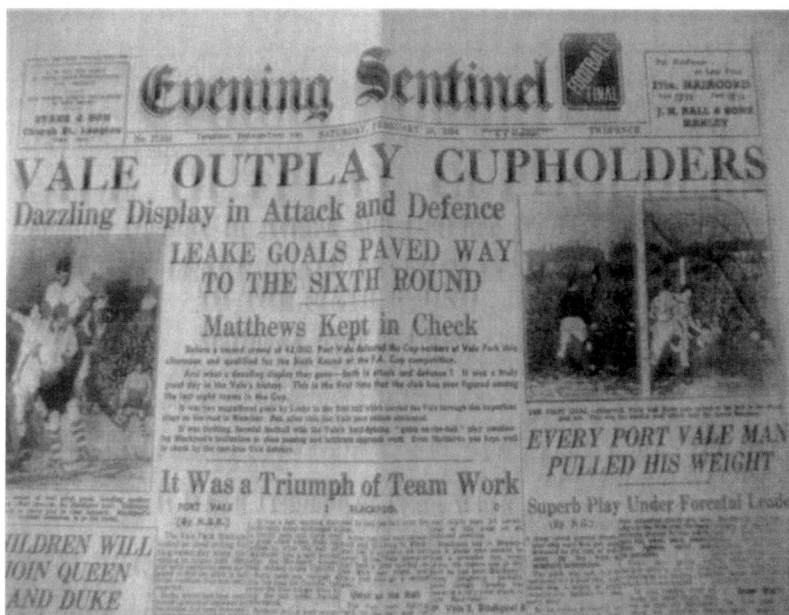

**How the 'Evening Sentinel' reported events that afternoon**

According to Albert Leake: 'Freddie Steele didn't see either of my goals as he was in the bath with a towel wrapped round his head for the entire 90 minutes! In fact, when we came off we could not get into the dressing room because Freddie had locked the door! I don't know why he was a manager because he couldn't watch a match."

Albert's weekly wage of £13 was supplemented by a win bonus of £2 and it was time to celebrate. Albert and his wife were not much for pubs and clubs but they joined a get together that night at the Victory Club, Smallthorne. His parents were members and all the family gathered to clap in the local hero. He was later presented with an engraved cigarette lighter by Sporting Record for their performance of the week.

Roy Sproson said: "We never entertained the idea of defeat and most teams, even those from the higher divisions that we met in the cup, were paralysed with fear at the prospect of playing us. We were a big physical team with a good number of six footers in the line-up and our wingers played deep when required."

Blackpool's Len Stephenson joined the Vale a year later, Jackie Mudie also joined the Vale in 1963, and Stanley Matthews became the club's general manager in 1965.

At the third round stage, Vale were 500-1 to win the FA Cup; after beating Blackpool they were down to 20-1. A Potteries four-man syndicate had backed Vale to win the FA Cup at the start of the competition with £100 and a superb faith!

A festive day was completed by news of the defeats of Vale's chief league challengers Gateshead and Barnsley. The Sentinel said that Vale fans spent the weekend discussing the prospects of a League and Cup double!

Ex-Vale player Ronnie Allen scored a hat-trick as West Brom beat Newcastle 3-2 in another of the day's fifth round ties.

Monday 22 February

The FA Cup quarter-final draw was made, with Port Vale at that stage for the first time ever.

Vale were drawn away for the fifth time in six rounds, this time to another third division team, Leyton Orient of Division 3 (South). The full draw was:

West Brom vs Hull City or Tottenham
Sheffield Wednesday vs Bolton or Portsmouth
Leyton Orient vs Port Vale
Leicester City vs Preston North End

It guaranteed a third division club in the FA Cup semi-finals, which had only happened once before, when Millwall did it in 1937.

**Tommy Cheadle gave the thumbs up sign when he heard from the 'Sentinel' that his team were drawn to play Leyton Orient away in the FA Cup sixth round. Others are Albert Leake, Roy Sproson, Freddie Steele, Reg Potts and Alderman GL Barber**

Leyton Orient immediately announced that the quarter final match would be all-ticket, with a limit of 30,000.

That evening's TV programme 'Newsreel' included some of the highlights of Saturday's cup tie. The receipts for the game were confirmed as being £7,290.

The Disciplinary Committee of the FA recommended that Cardiff be ordered to post warning notices on their ground and print similar warnings in the club programme, following incidents at the fourth round game against Vale when snowballing of the referee took place!

**Cartoon which featured in the 'Evening Sentinel' on the Monday after the Vale win over Blackpool**

Wednesday 24 February

**York City 0 Port Vale 1**

Vale selected the same team that had beaten Blackpool. The game kicked off at 3pm and York twice went close, Billy Fenton heading the ball over the bar and King making a splendid save from Johnny Linaker, but Vale took the lead after 39 minutes when Griffiths sent in a beautiful cross from almost at the corner flag and Hayward drove the ball into the net with his left foot. Hayward netted again in the second half but was adjudged offside, then Linaker hit the bar for York, but Vale held on for their first league win of 1954.

Vale – King, Turner, Potts, Mullard, Cheadle, Sproson, Askey, Leake, Hayward, Griffiths, Cunliffe
Att: 7,131

## Thursday 25 February

President Neguib, Egypt's 'popular dictator', resigned and was replaced by Vice-Premier Colonel Nasser who proclaimed a state of emergency throughout Egypt.

Train tickets to Leyton Orient went on sale at £1.13; trains would depart from Tunstall, Burslem, Cobridge, Hanley, Kidsgrove, Longport, Etruria, Stoke, Fenton, Longton, Normacot, Meir and Blythe Bridge.

Pat Coates of Birches Head was chosen as the Vale's queen at the Northern Area Supporters Club dance. Five years later she became the wife of Vale professional goalkeeper John Poole.

## Friday 26 February

It was announced that a feature on the Port Vale and Leyton Orient football clubs would be broadcast on the BBC Light Programme on 12 March, the eve of their sixth round FA Cup meeting. Players and other personalities were to take part.

## Saturday 27 February

**Port Vale 2 Chesterfield 2**

In total in all of their previous 20 home games Vale had conceded just ONE goal! This run consisted of the last four home games of the 1952/53 season together with two FA Cup games and fourteen league games so far during 1953/54. Billy Burnett of Hartlepools United on 5 September was the only opponent who had breached the Vale rearguard during that time, from 4 April 1953 when they drew 1-1 with Oldham Athletic until this game against Chesterfield. One goal conceded in 1,855 minutes of football! No wonder the Vale defence had acquired the nickname 'The Steele Curtain'. It was a run of almost 11 months.

The game began in difficult conditions and falling snow. After 18 minutes Hayward hit a fierce drive which rebounded off the diving

Ronnie Powell and Cunliffe crashed the ball against the underside of the bar and into the net. Vale went into half-time 2-0 ahead courtesy of a goal in the 36th minute when, from a deep corner by Askey, Griffiths hit the ball on the volley with a shot which flew into the net like a rocket.

Chesterfield pulled a goal back after 51 minutes when George Smith's shot deflected off a defender's back and flew out of King's reach and into the roof of the net. Vale had gone an incredible 1,293 minutes of play without conceding a goal at home since Burnett's goal for Hartlepools. In an end to end game during which it continued to snow Vale only went another 26 minutes before conceding again as Chesterfield equalised when Ken Whiteside headed in a cross from Pat Keating. There were further chances and near misses at both ends and King and Powell made many fine saves. It was the first time Vale had conceded two goals in a league game at home since 30 August 1952 when they beat Rochdale 5-2, a run of 35 home league games.

Vale – King, Turner, Potts, Mullard, Cheadle, Sproson, Askey, Leake, Hayward, Griffiths, Cunliffe

Att: 19,886

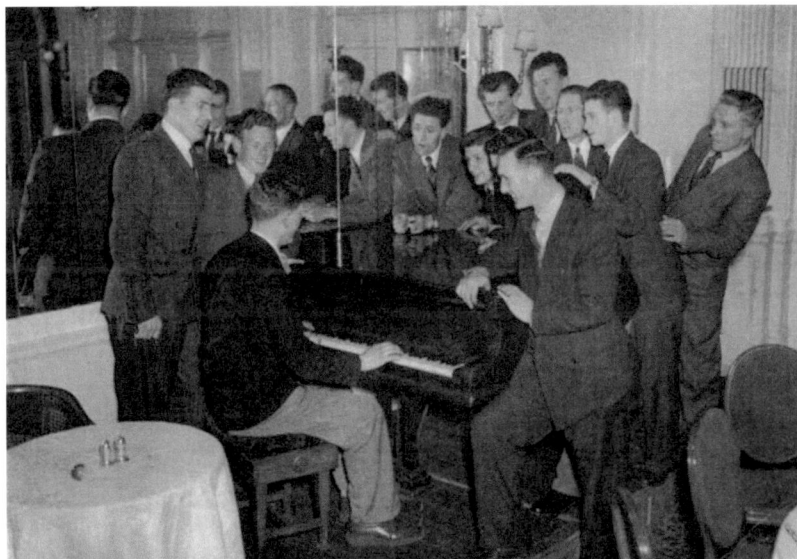

**The players have a celebratory sing song around the piano**

League table:

|  | P | W | D | L | F | A | PTS |
|---|---|---|---|---|---|---|---|
| PORT VALE | 31 | 20 | 8 | 3 | 50 | 14 | 48 |
| Gateshead | 33 | 16 | 10 | 7 | 60 | 37 | 42 |
| Bradford City | 33 | 19 | 4 | 10 | 50 | 37 | 42 |
| Barnsley | 32 | 16 | 8 | 8 | 51 | 39 | 40 |
| Scunthorpe U | 32 | 13 | 12 | 7 | 50 | 42 | 38 |
| Mansfield T | 34 | 13 | 9 | 12 | 64 | 55 | 35 |

# March

Monday 1 March

The United States tested the Hydrogen bomb on Bikini atoll in the Pacific Ocean.

Limoges FC of France invited the Vale over for an end of season tour in May. The board were going to discuss it in due course.

Wednesday 3 March

Heavy snowstorms swept the country, in some areas the worst of the winter. JW Topliss from Grimsby, who was down to referee the Leyton Orient vs Port Vale sixth round FA Cup tie, collapsed after arriving at White Hart Lane to take charge of the Tottenham vs Bolton First Division match, and was taken to hospital.

Ethel Shaw, of 3 Buckmaster Avenue Newcastle, was chosen as the first Lady Mayor of Newcastle-under-Lyme.

Thursday 4 March

Tickets for the FA Cup tie at Leyton Orient were to be sold at Saturday's Cheshire League reserve team game against Hyde United. After meeting '100 club', season ticket and Supporters' Club commitments, the remainder of the tickets would be available. Supporters Clubs got about one ticket for every four members and had to have ballots to decide who would get one.

The club made similar arrangements as for fifth round tickets. Prices were 15p ground and 25p paddock and the Vale allocation of 7,500 was well below the expected demand, although it was the maximum allowed, being 25% of capacity.

Saturday 6 March

An hour before the gates were due to open for the reserve game at 2pm, queues stretched three and four deep over 100 yards from the Hamil Road turnstiles along the Lorne Street fence. Crowds were cheerful in spite of a soaking from the morning rain.

The first arrival at Vale Park had been Mr Arthur Woodward of 1A, Glover Street, Birches Head, who had travelled to the ground straight from his night shift at Sneyd Colliery and arrived at 6am, eight hours before the gates were due to be opened. He headed the queue at the 15p turnstiles.

The reserve match with Hyde United finished 3-3 with Hulligan, Willdigg and Barber (pen) scoring for Vale. Later the club announced that their allocation of tickets for the sixth round FA Cup tie had been completely sold out and that hundreds of postal applications would be returned.

It had been agreed that, if the game at Leyton Orient ended in a draw, the replay would be at Vale Park on the following Monday.

**Tranmere Rovers 1 Port Vale 3**

Alec Stock, the manager of Leyton Orient, was at Prenton Park to see the Valiants take on Tranmere. Vale had two Directors watching the O's play Walsall. In those days directors were often used to spy on the opposition!

In the 20th minute Rovers took the lead when Bill Bainbridge crashed the ball into the Vale net after a left wing raid by the home side. Vale promptly hit back two minutes later after Mullard's free kick was turned by Hayward to Griffiths who swiftly hooked the ball into the corner. After a spell of pressure in which Vale laid siege to the Tranmere goal, Hayward headed home from Askey's centre in the last minute of the first half. Five minutes from time a shot from Don Woan hit the Vale crossbar but within seconds Hayward clinched the points by shooting home, again from a pass by Askey. It completed Vale's fourth double of the season so far.

Vale – King, Turner, Potts, Mullard, Cheadle, Sproson, Askey, Leake, Hayward, Griffiths, Cunliffe
Att: 9,946

Sunday 7 March

1,200 53p Cup-tie tickets were stolen from the Leyton Orient offices. The raiders also took the club's records and £600 in cash after blowing open two safes.

96

## Monday 8 March

A warning was issued by the Chief Constable that some of the Cup tie tickets stolen from the Leyton Orient offices the previous day may be offered for sale in the Potteries.

The FA decided that Mr BM Griffiths of Newport would referee the cup match as Mr Topliss had still not recovered sufficiently to do so.

Eight special trains were to convey fans from the Potteries to London on Saturday. The team were to travel on the 11:15am train on Friday morning, returning on the 6:30pm from Euston on Saturday.

Leyton Orient were training all week in the Kent seaside town of Westgate-on-Sea but Vale stuck to their normal routine and stayed at home.

## Thursday 11 March

Ken Fish, despite being 40, was one of the fittest trainers in the country, not only setting the training routine but also taking part! He also played in the Midland mid-week league team to help the young players and on one occasion turned out for the reserves in a Cheshire League match.

Another indication of Vale's superstitions was that a local outfitter had presented the team with a complete new outfit but they refused to wear it while they were on a winning streak.

## Friday 12 March

Over 100 supporters lined the platform at Stoke station to see the team off!

That evening the team saw Arthur Askey in the West End show 'The Love Match'.

Colin Askey remembered, "The night before the game we stayed in a top hotel in London overnight and all the squad went to the theatre. The comedian Arthur Askey was the compere and because we had made a name for ourselves that season he invited us all up

97

on stage. When he got to my name he hesitated for a moment and then said 'Hello son, meet your father!' We also went backstage and met his daughter, the actress Anthea Askey."

**Vale players arriving in London for their sixth round FA Cup-tie at Leyton Orient**

Saturday 13 March

**FA Cup sixth round;**
**Leyton Orient 0 Port Vale 1**

Special trains left the Potteries at intervals between 6:25 and 10:00am and were returning between 10:30pm on Saturday night and 2:40am on Sunday morning.

There were 250 police officers on duty around Brisbane Road looking for stolen or forged tickets. The stolen tickets had been officially reprinted but with a secret mark. Every approach road to the ground was sealed off and only those with genuine tickets were allowed through.

Before the match the team hung their big black and white rosette, with a silver horseshoe, in the dressing room. Around it were scores of 'Good Luck' telegrams.

The pitch was uneven and with hardly any grass apart from in the corners. Vale were on the radio for the second time in less than

98

24 hours as the match was chosen by the BBC for the Light Programme 'Match of the Day' commentary, following a documentary broadcast the previous evening. In those days Leyton Orient's colours were blue shirts and white shorts, whereas nowadays they are red and white.

After 19 minutes Askey's corner was headed down by Hayward and Leake promptly flashed a low drive past David Groombridge into the far corner of the net.

**Ken Griffiths (centre) watches a shot from Albert Leake (left) enter the Leyton Orient net for the only goal of the game**

A Hayward shot was then saved by the home keeper and, after 30 minutes, Cunliffe sent a fierce drive over the bar. George Poulton, Orient's left winger, was then injured and carried off on a stretcher. Griffiths then skimmed the bar with a shot and Cunliffe headed an Askey cross onto the roof of the net before King made two good saves and also required treatment.

Poulton resumed when the teams came out for the second half, and Groombridge and Griffiths were then injured in the 47th minute when the goalkeeper dived at the Vale player's feet.

Both carried on after receiving attention but the Vale playmaker had received quite a bad knee injury. Mullard then had a good effort saved and, just before the end, King brilliantly turned a rising drive from Poulton over the bar.

**Ken Griffiths injures his knee in challenging Groombridge for the ball – a challenge that would have greater repercussions later for Ken**

When the final whistle sounded, Vale had become only the second team ever from the third division to reach the FA Cup semi-finals, and the first ever from Division 3 North.

Vale – King, Turner, Potts, Mullard, Cheadle, Sproson, Askey, Leake, Hayward, Griffiths, Cunliffe
Att: 31,000

Ray King remembered, "The night before the game my foot swelled up with an infection and it was only thanks to the efforts of our trainer Ken Fish that I was passed fit to play. Even then I had to wear a boot two sizes too big that was borrowed from the home team! I had actually played for Leyton for a short spell just after the war, but it was nothing like the atmosphere generated during this game. It was electric, and tremendous to play in.

**Ray King confidently catches a Leyton Orient cross. The whole Vale defence is featured in this photo.**

In the last minute I remember I had to tip an effort over the bar from Poulton and the media hailed it as the save of the season. It was very flattering to read that but I think it had more to do with it being the last minute of such a big occasion that made it stand out for people."

Roy Sproson said: 'This was a terrible game to play in. Both teams were nervous and, on a bumpy pitch, the ball was never still. It was whacked from end to end and one goal from us was enough to settle it.'

Colin Askey said: "There was little between the teams and, although we went ahead, it was Ray King who kept us in it with a fantastic save right at the end. As soon as their lad hit it, I thought 'this is going in', but Ray somehow kept it out and we were into the last four of the FA Cup. Dreamland."

After the game a sugar cigarettes firm offered Ray King £6 to use his name and photograph in their adverts

The other quarter final results were:

Leicester City 1 Preston North End 1
Sheffield Wednesday 1 Bolton Wanderers 1
West Bromwich Albion 3 Tottenham Hotspur 0

**The lucky rosette sent by a fan adorning Roy Sproson**

Monday 15 March

Albert Leake's wife had been at the game on Saturday and seen him score the winning goal, but they had travelled back separately, and her husband was back home an hour before her!

It was also revealed that one of the special trains carrying Vale supporters to the match had arrived at Leyton station three minutes after the game had kicked off and 90 minutes behind schedule. The supporters on that train then had to get to the ground and, by the time they had done so, they had missed the Vale's goal. The train had started from Tunstall at 8:30 and left Stoke station on time after

102

calling at Burslem, Cobridge, Hanley and Etruria but developed engine trouble and gradually lost time.

There wasn't much rest for Vale after their heroics on Saturday as they had another league game the following Monday afternoon at 3:15.

Roy Sproson said: "The realisation that we, a Third Division side, were in the semi-finals frightened us a little. Nobody really wanted to play before the big match for fear of being injured."

News of the FA Cup semi-final draw reached the Vale players by a telephone call from the Sentinel office to the Vale Park boardroom just before the league game with Halifax Town was due to start. The draw came out like this:

West Bromwich Albion vs Port Vale
Leicester City or Preston North End vs Sheffield Wednesday or Bolton Wanderers

Vale could be considered very unlucky as, at the time of the draw, West Brom were top of Division 1. The other two eventual semi-finalists, Preston and Sheffield Wednesday, were 11th and 15th respectively. At the end of the season West Brom were second, Preston 11th and Sheffield Wednesday 19th. The Vale's semi-final was to be staged at Villa Park, with the other game being at Maine Road, Manchester.

## Port Vale 2 Halifax Town 0

Ken Griffiths missed the match due to the knee injury sustained at Leyton Orient and was replaced by Derek Tomkinson. Before the game started the crowd enthusiastically cheered the Vale players in appreciation of their history making cup achievement.

A Hayward header and a low drive from Cunliffe were Vale's best two efforts of an uninspiring first half. Things picked up after the interval and, after 53 minutes, David McCormick dived to push a Hayward header onto a post. After 76 minutes Vale got the breakthrough when Sproson's free-kick found Leake who crashed a left foot drive through a crowded goalmouth into the net. Five minutes later Askey hooked in a left foot shot to seal the points. Before the game ended Hayward and Mullard were limping.

Vale – King, Turner, Potts, Mullard, Cheadle, Sproson, Askey, Leake, Hayward, Tomkinson, Cunliffe
Att: 10,533

The programme for the game was a single card, priced at 2d because at such a busy time there wasn't enough time to print a proper programme. This also applied to the home games v Accrington Mansfield and Bradford City, although the latter was a four page card

Wednesday 17 March

It was announced that tickets for the semi-final would be sold at Vale's reserve team home game with Mossley the following Saturday. Each spectator would be allocated a 13p ticket for the terraces or a 30p one for the paddock. Seat tickets were £1.25 and were reserved for season ticket holders. Hundreds of postal applications had already been received but would not be considered

**Colin Askey scores the second goal v Halifax**

Because of injuries and knocks received in the previous two games, Vale made sweeping changes for the team to visit Carlisle on the coming Saturday:

Ray King – painful foot and injured side – to be replaced by Ray Hancock
Ken Griffiths – swollen knee – to be replaced by Derek Tomkinson
Basil Hayward – pulled thigh muscle – to be replaced by Len Barber
Stan Turner – bruising – to be replaced by Jim Elsby
Colin Askey – bruising – to be replaced by Mick Hulligan
Dickie Cunliffe – bruising – to be replaced by Alan Bennett

It would be the first appearance of the season for Hancock, Barber and Bennett. Pat Willdigg was to travel as reserve. Vale were to leave by coach on the Friday.

Saturday 20 March

**Some of the queues for FA Cup semi-final tickets at Vale Park**

Mile long queues stretched four and five deep all round the forecourt of Vale Park and up Hamil Road when the gates were opened for the sale of FA Cup semi-final tickets. A second queue for 13p tickets lined the whole length of the Lorne Street fence up to

Bycars road and a third for 30p tickets twisted around the car park on the Railway terrace side for more than half a mile.

**More huge queues**

About 100 supporters per minute passed through the ten turnstiles, but the queues did not diminish as hundreds flocked in on the fifty special buses running a shuttle service to and from Burslem. An hour after the gates opened the queue for 13p tickets still stretched all the way up Hamil Road to within a few yards of High Lane. The crowds were estimated at 40,000 but not all of them managed to get into the ground.

Dawn had not broken when the first enthusiasts had arrived in pouring rain. Some had gone to the ground the previous evening but heavy rain had driven them away in the early hours of the morning. The ex-Manchester United and Congleton Town centre-forward Tom Beswick, who had hitch-hiked from Congleton, started the queue at one of the 13p turnstiles at 6am.

Altogether 30,000 passed through the turnstiles, making the reserve game against Mossley the Vale's largest 'attendance' of the season! Only a few thousand stayed to watch the game though, which ended in a 1-1 draw. The "sold out" signs were posted around 2.30pm, and quite a few of the disappointed fans immediately made their way to Birmingham, as tickets were to go on general sale the next day at both the Hawthorns, West Brom's ground, and at Villa Park itself between 10am and noon.

It was also announced that, if the semi-final ended in a draw, the replay would be held at Stoke City's Victoria Ground the following Thursday, 1 April with a 3pm kick off.

ROW    SEAT

# A 1

---

**F.A. CHALLENGE CUP COMPETITION**

## SEMI-FINAL TIE REPLAY

**AT VICTORIA GROUND, Stoke-on-Trent**

### THURSDAY, APRIL 1st, 1954

# WEST BROMWICH A.

*versus*

# PORT VALE

KICK-OFF 3 p.m.

---

# Boothen Stand

# Block B - - £1. 1. 0.

(Including Tax)

W. C. WILLIAMS, *Secretary.*
**STOKE CITY F.C. (1908) CO., LTD.**

**Ticket printed in advance for a possible semi-final replay, which would have been played at the Victoria Ground, Stoke**

### Carlisle United 0 Port Vale 0

Ken Fish was in charge of the Vale team at Carlisle as Freddie Steele and the rested players were watching West Brom defeat Blackpool at the Hawthorns. Vale played in red and white striped shirts and black shorts. The under-strength team got a hard earned point in an even game in which both goalkeepers Ray Hancock, making his first appearance of the season for Vale, and Jimmy McLaren for the Cumbrians, made several excellent saves.

107

As Carlisle had not yet begun the rebuilding of the stand gutted by fire the previous year, the Vale players had to change at the local public baths in the town centre and arrived at Brunton Park a few minutes before the kick off to enter the field straight from their coach!

At centre-forward for Carlisle was Alan Ashman who later managed the club to promotion to Division 1 for the only time in its history in 1974. He also managed West Bromwich Albion to an FA Cup win in 1968.

Hulligan almost scored for Vale in the first minute but his shot was well saved, then Ashman had a header ruled out for offside. Barber and Hulligan had further near misses for Vale and Bennett worked well on the wing. Ashman continued to be the main threat for the home side but the Vale reserve players had acquitted themselves well.

Vale – Hancock, Elsby, Potts, Mullard, Cheadle, Sproson, Hulligan, Leake, Barber, Tomkinson, Bennett
Att: 9,995

It was announced that the following railway stations would be open until 9:30pm every day for the sale of tickets to Witton station next to Villa Park: Hanley, Burslem, Tunstall, Cobridge, Bucknall, Newcastle and Silverdale.

Wednesday 24 March

Roy Sproson said: "The build up to the game against West Bromwich at Villa Park was wonderful. Pressmen who previously had not probably even heard of Port Vale trained with us and camped on the doorstep. We had good luck letters from all over the world and the usual pleas for tickets.

I must be the only player on record to lose money from an FA Cup semi-final. In addition to my two complimentaries, I bought a couple of 13p tickets for friends. One of them failed to turn up so I lost the cash! Furthermore, the players received just our basic wage for that game."

Vale's only doubtful starter for the semi-final was Ken Griffiths with a knee injury picked up in the win at Leyton Orient. Griffiths was examined by Dr EF Higgins, the club's honorary medical officer.

108

## Thursday 25 March

Griffiths was continuing training and having constant treatment. The plan was for him to have treatment up to the morning of the match and then have a thorough fitness test. In view of the fact that no substitutions were allowed in those days, he would only play if 100% fit. Tomkinson and Elsby were to travel as reserves.

Ken Griffiths said: "I had reached the stage where I was having treatment seven days a week and Ken Fish would go to the Vale Cafe in Hamil Road to fetch my Sunday lunch so that he could keep me on the treatment table."

The other ten first teamers were fit and had their last practice match before the semi-final. On Friday afternoon they were to travel to a 'secret' destination outside Birmingham, which turned out to be Droitwich. On the morning of the match they were to travel to Villa Park to look at the pitch, then rest in a 'quiet and guarded' dressing room. They were to return to the Potteries by coach after the match with a halt on the way for an evening meal.

## Friday 26 March

The team set out shortly before 3pm and took with them a toy black cat mascot embroidered in white with the names of the players, sent by Mrs Hewitt of Burslem who provided the giant black and white rosette which they took with them to Leyton Orient for luck. They had also received 'Good Luck' telegrams from as far away as Korea and New Zealand. The players were to see a stage show that evening.

While the Vale were trying to become the first team from Division 3 ever to reach an FA Cup final, West Brom were attempting to become the first team since 1897 to do the Football League Championship and FA Cup double. Both teams were top of their respective divisions.

## Saturday 27 March

Over 100 coaches and 14 special trains set off from the Potteries to Villa Park that Saturday morning. Most of the rest of the supporters went by car but a few hardy souls even ventured by bicycle!

Among the first arrivals at Villa Park was a man of 75 who had come 3,000 miles to cheer the Vale to Wembley. He was Mr Isaiah Birks, son of a Fenton builder, who had been following Vale's fortunes from Trenton, New Jersey, USA.

**Albert Leake's family leaves Smallthorne for Villa Park**

The first train load of 760 fans pulled out of Burslem at 8:20. According to the Sentinel many Burslem husbands had the understanding farewell from their wives of 'See you Monday morning, duck!'

In the meantime, Ken Griffiths, Freddie Steele and Ken Fish went to a sports ground two miles from the team hotel for a final fitness test. After the test Griffiths turned to Freddie Steele and said "I am sorry but my knee still hurts and I cannot honestly say that I am fit". The manager told Griffiths to go and gather his thoughts, and he just sat on a wall and cried.

Ken Griffiths said: "Ken Fish our trainer was almost as disappointed as me because nobody had worked harder to keep me playing."

110

**Some of the first arrivals in Birmingham for the semi-final**

The club's medical officer said that he could give Griffiths an injection to get him through the game (presumably cortisone), but that if he got a knock on it he could well be crippled for life. He couldn't take that risk even for such a huge game, and Vale therefore had to make their first change of the entire FA Cup run: Derek Tomkinson was brought into the team to replace Griffiths. Amazingly, it was the only FA Cup tie that Tomkinson ever played for Vale.

West Brom had been drawn at home in every round, with the semi-final being very close to their home as well. Vale on the other hand had been drawn at home just the once.

In those days the pre-match entertainment for big games was a marching band. At Villa Park that day the Band of the Royal Warwickshire Regiment played before the match, and their numbers included 'Colonel Bogey on Parade', 'Thumbelina' and 'Ugly Duckling'!

There was an official programme and no less than five different unofficial 'pirate' programmes for the match!

THE FOOTBALL ASSOCIATION
CHALLENGE CUP

# SEMI-FINAL TIE

*Photograph by A. Walker & Son, West Bromwich.*

## WEST BROMWICH ALBION
v.
## PORT VALE

At VILLA PARK, BIRMINGHAM
**SATURDAY, MARCH 27th 1954**
KICK-OFF 3 p.m.

OFFICIAL PROGRAMME ISSUED BY ASTON VILLA F.C.
**SIXPENCE**

J. Goodman & Sons (Printers) Ltd., Birmingham, 4.

**The official programme**

West Brom were at full strength and the teams lined up as follows:

Port Vale – King, Turner, Potts, Mullard, Cheadle, Sproson, Askey, Leake, Hayward, Tomkinson, Cunliffe.
West Bromwich Albion – Heath, Rickaby, Millard, Dudley, Dugdale, Barlow, Griffin, Ryan, Allen, Nicholls, Lee.

**The kick off at Villa Park**

## FA Cup semi-final;
## West Bromwich Albion 2 Port Vale 1

Tommy Cheadle won the toss and, after Albion had kicked off, Vale won the first corner but Cunliffe's kick was cleared. Frank Griffin then sent a fierce drive just wide for Albion. A few minutes later, Potts lobbed the ball into the West Brom goalmouth but it was cleared after a scramble, then King turned away a 20 yard effort from Allen. Vale almost scored after 29 minutes when Norman Heath made a desperate save from a header by Tomkinson. Jimmy Dugdale then had to head back to his 'keeper to intercept another dangerous Vale move, before King magnificently turned over a terrific drive from Griffin.

After 40 minutes Cunliffe put the ball into the Albion goalmouth and, after a hectic scramble involving Leake, Tomkinson, Hayward, Cunliffe and the West Brom defence, Leake succeeded in forcing the ball into the net. A few minutes later the referee blew for half-time with Vale 1-0 ahead.

The second half began in an end to end fashion but there were no clear cut chances until the 62nd minute when Dudley, out on the Albion right flank, sent a long high ball into the middle. Cheadle, bustled by Allen, just about grazed the ball with his head, which dropped into the goalmouth and rolled into the corner of the net, catching King unawares.

**West Brom's first goal sneaks into the corner of the net**

In the 65<sup>th</sup> minute Stan Turner clashed with George Lee in the Vale penalty area ending with the West Brom man clutching his stomach prone on the ground. The referee said play on, but a section of the crowd booed Turner from then on.

Allen then hit a drive against the foot of a post, before, in the 70<sup>th</sup> minute Lee escaped from Turner and Cheadle, in trying to catch the Albion winger up from behind, fell with the player near the edge of the penalty area. The Vale players claimed that Lee had handled the ball in rounding Turner. After the tackle, Cheadle fell on his back outside the area and Lee stumbled to the ground inside the box. The referee was prompt with his decision to award a penalty and thought it unnecessary to consult his linesman. Was the referee trying to make up for the incident five minutes earlier?

**Tommy Cheadle's tackle on Lee for which the referee awarded a penalty – you make your own mind up!**

Former Vale striker Allen made no mistake from the spot with a hard drive into the bottom left hand corner of the net. West Brom had previously only had one penalty that season, against Burnley, and Allen had missed!

Five minutes before the end Cunliffe went close to equalising with a drive that went just wide of the post and then, a minute later, Leake netted but was given offside. Colin Askey maintained that he pulled the ball back so that offside wasn't an issue, but disallowed it was. Vale made a fight of it right to the end with Albion keeper Heath in action several times.

The attendance was 68,221 – the highest gate ever to watch a game involving the Vale - and the receipts were £20,086.60, a record at the time for an FA Cup semi-final.

**Ronnie Allen scores from the penalty spot to put West Brom 2-1 in front**

Tommy Cheadle said, "I wouldn't say that the penalty decision wasn't a foul, but it definitely wasn't in the area. We were comfortable at the time, and it's such a disappointing way to go out."

Fenton born West Brom striker Ronnie Allen, whose ticket allocation included one for his father, a staunch Vale supporter, said that lining up for the penalty was the most nerve-wracking moment of his career. "Everything flashed through my mind as I lined up to take the kick. Port Vale were my old club and the one that started my career – if I had have missed it people would have said I did it deliberately, and if I scored then Potteries fans would say I should never have taken a penalty against the Vale. As I ran to take it I just aimed for a photographer lying prone behind the net and hit it as hard as I could. If it wasn't for the net, his camera would have been smashed to smithereens!
I did get some letters saying that I shouldn't have taken it! Before the draw for the semi's I dreamed of a West Brom v Vale final, but it wasn't to be."

Stan Turner explained what happened with his tangle with Lee five minutes before the penalty. "It was an accident, a pure accident, and I wrote to him to apologise. We both went for the ball and I fell on my back with my feet in the air. Lee jumped over me and I accidentally caught him in the stomach, but no way was it deliberate, however bad it looked."

Ray King said: "West Brom were top of the First Division at the time, but we were playing out of our skins and we should have gone through. We were devastated after the game. I guess it was just fate, it wasn't meant to be – but that doesn't make it any easier to take. They score two dodgy goals and we should have been going to Wembley. Their first goal was a fluke of an own goal which came off the back of Tommy Cheadle's head. Poor Tommy was as deaf as a door post and I was shouting at him to leave it, but he didn't hear me and he slipped and put it in the net. I was a bit annoyed that some of the match reports in the papers the next day blamed me for that goal because they didn't know the full story.

Also, the penalty was never a penalty; the foul was easily outside the box. Looking at the television replays of the incident, even in grainy black and white, you can see that is obvious. Ronnie Allen, who used to play for Vale, took the penalty. He used to practice them against me in those days, so I knew exactly where he was going to hit it, and he knew that I knew. When he stepped up, though, he hammered it right into the corner. I got my fingertips to it, but it was hit too hard and flew into the net – and that was that, we were out."

Colin Askey said: "Ken Griffiths missed the semi-final. Derek Tomkinson came in for him and did a good job, but the balance of the side was disrupted. We just didn't play as well as we knew we could. Fate dealt us a cruel blow that day. West Brom's winner was a hotly disputed penalty that Ronnie Allen put away. I had a clear view of it and the foul was committed outside the box. Television evidence merely confirmed this. Then with us trailing 2-1 with two minutes to go I slipped the ball to Albert Leake who scored. The heads of the West Brom players went down. We were celebrating, but the referee then blew for offside. We couldn't believe it. We were devastated. Even the West Brom team thought it was a legitimate goal; they hadn't even appealed for offside. Two minutes later we were sitting in the dressing room shell shocked."

Roy Sproson said: 'We were a big, strong, physical side and quickly settled down against Albion. By half-time we seriously thought the game was as good as over. At the time we did not know what it was like to lose and the thought never occurred to us. We were convinced, in fact, that we could not be beaten.

What really upset us was the goal which we had disallowed. Colin Askey beat two men in a great run to the by-line before pulling the ball back for Albert Leake to crack home, but it was ruled offside. That upset us even more than the penalty."

West Brom's Jimmy Dugdale also played against the Vale for Aston Villa at Vale Park in February 1960, when the crowd was a ground record 49,768, so he appeared for the opposition in Vale's biggest attendances both home and away. Roy Sproson and Albert Leake also played in both games

After the match, in Vale's dressing room, Freddie Steele took off the lucky black and white socks he'd worn for about three months and threw them into the washing basket. A few minutes later he was scrambling to get them out again after he was asked to do a TV interview and had no others to wear!

Preston North End beat Sheffield Wednesday 2-0 in the other semi-final at Maine Road, Manchester.

On the same day, the Grand National was won by Royal Tan by a neck from Tudor Line in one of the closest ever finishes to the race.

Sunday 28 March

Even though greatly disappointed from the previous day, the Vale players and staff appeared at the Wesley Place Methodist Church in Tunstall for a Sportsman's Service.

After the disappointment of the semi-final defeat, Vale had to face up to four games the following week:

Monday – vs an All Star XI in a testimonial at Vale Park. The proceeds of this game were for the members of the Vale playing staff who had given long and valuable service. The match had been arranged by some North Staffordshire businessmen.
Tuesday – vs Accrington (h)
Thursday – vs Bradford City (h)

118

Saturday – vs Grimsby Town (a) – the team were to leave on the Friday

**Ray King about to read a lesson at the church service**

Monday 29 March

Vale President Tom Flint died aged 68. He had been ill for a long time at his home Royana, Shooter's Hill, Rough Close. The elder of his two daughters was Mrs FM Pinfold whose husband was a Director of Port Vale. From the time he had arrived in the area from Manchester, where he was born, Tom was a supporter of the Vale and helped to raise funds for the club. In his younger days in Manchester he had been a player and a referee. He was a sack and bag merchant with premises in Hope Street, Hanley and later in Tunstall. He became a Director in 1931, then Vice-Chairman, then Chairman between 1940-1946. Ill health caused him to relinquish the Chairmanship and he resigned from the board in 1949. He had served for 13 years as an Independent on the City Council, resigning for health reasons in 1946.

He never knew the result of the FA Cup semi-final.

The Vale players carried his coffin into church at his funeral at Meir Heath. In his memory his family donated the clock that went over the tunnel which is still there today.

Vale played an 'All Star' XI at Vale Park in a testimonial match which kicked off at 5:15pm. Not since 6 October 1952 had Vale been beaten at home but they were in this game and the scorer of the two goals which beat them was none other than the Vale's manager, Freddie Steele! Steele was centre forward for the 'All Star XI' who won 2-1 against a Vale team, which included eight of the FA Cup semi-final line-up from just two days earlier. The visitors comprised former players, many of them past internationals. Barber gave Vale the lead after 20 minutes, heading in a cross by Hulligan, but then Steele (26 and 39 minutes) became the first player to beat King twice in a match that season!

Vale team: King, Elsby, Potts, Mullard, Cheadle, Sproson, Hulligan, Leake, Barber, Tomkinson, Cunliffe.

All Stars team:

Frank Swift – ex-Manchester City goalkeeper
Bert Sproston – trainer at Bolton Wanderers
Andy Beattie – manager of Huddersfield Town
Bill Corkhill – manager of Scunthorpe United
Les McDowall – manager of Manchester City
Joe Mercer – still playing for Arsenal
Sammy Crooks – manager of Shrewsbury Town
Raich Carter – manager of Leeds United
Freddie Steele
Tim Ward – manager of Barnsley
Peter Doherty – manager of Doncaster Rovers

Matt Busby and Stanley Matthews had been in the All Stars squad but had to pull out due to club commitments.

The attendance was 11,500.

Peter Doherty had played twice for the Vale during the war as a guest and Raich Carter's father, Robert, played almost 100 games for Vale in the early part of the 20<sup>th</sup> century.

120

<u>Tuesday 30 March</u>

**Port Vale 1 Accrington Stanley 0**

The Vale Park pitch was in a greasy state following the previous day's rain and testimonial match. Barber replaced the injured Hayward and Griffiths returned for Tomkinson, although he did not appear to be fully recovered from the knee injury which had kept him out of the semi-final. In fact, he then played only one of the following seven games, so the injury was still affecting him greatly. In a match of few chances the winning goal came two minutes before half-time when Leake chipped the ball in to Griffiths who flicked it square to Cunliffe to flash in a first time drive. In the last minute Vale were awarded a penalty for handball but Barber sent the spot kick over the bar. It was only Vale's second penalty of the season and they had missed them both.

It was the Vale's lowest gate of the season, but the supporters must have been low on funds after the previous two months!

Vale – King, Turner, Potts, Mullard, Cheadle, Sproson, Askey, Leake, Barber, Griffiths, Cunliffe
Att: 9,367

League table:

|              | P  | W  | D  | L  | F  | A  | PTS |
|--------------|----|----|----|----|----|----|-----|
| PORT VALE    | 35 | 23 | 9  | 3  | 56 | 15 | 55  |
| Barnsley     | 38 | 21 | 8  | 9  | 66 | 44 | 50  |
| Gateshead    | 38 | 19 | 10 | 9  | 67 | 46 | 48  |
| Bradford C   | 37 | 22 | 4  | 11 | 54 | 39 | 48  |
| Scunthorpe U | 38 | 15 | 14 | 9  | 59 | 52 | 44  |
| Mansfield T  | 39 | 16 | 10 | 13 | 78 | 62 | 42  |

121

# April

Thursday 1 April

Vale's next game in a busy week was against Bradford City, whose player-manager was none other than Ivor Powell, the Vale's player-manager immediately before Freddie Steele took over in late 1951. Powell also managed Carlisle United and Bath City and entered the Guinness Book of Records in 2006 for being the world's oldest coach at 90 years of age with Team Bath! He was awarded the MBE in 2008 for services to sport and died aged 96 in November 2012. Before losing 2-1 at Scunthorpe the previous Saturday, Bradford City had won nine games in a row, seven of them 1-0.

**Port Vale 3 Bradford City 0**

Despite making an appearance against Accrington, Griffiths was out injured again for this game, and was replaced by Tomkinson. Barber continued to deputise for the injured Hayward at centre-forward. After a quiet first half, Vale took the lead on 51 minutes when Tomkinson hooked the ball over Geoff Smith after the City keeper had fisted out a shot from Barber. Five minutes later, Smith tipped a Leake header onto the bar and Barber scored from the rebound. Vale completed the scoring six minutes from time when Tomkinson headed home a Leake cross.

Vale – King, Turner, Potts, Mullard, Cheadle, Sproson, Askey, Tomkinson, Barber, Leake, Cunliffe
Att: 18,418

AW Luty (Leeds) was appointed FA Cup final referee. He had refereed the Vale's second round tie at Southport.

Saturday 3 April

England won 4-2 against Scotland at Hampden Park in a World Cup qualifier. Ronnie Allen and Johnny Nicholls from the West Brom team, who had beaten Vale the previous Saturday, played for England and both scored, Nicholls on his 23rd birthday. George Farm and Allan Brown, who had played for Blackpool in the fifth round at Vale Park, played for Scotland. Farm was in goal and Brown scored one of Scotland's goals. The attendance was 134,544!

122

**Grimsby Town 2 Port Vale 2**

Vale were unchanged from the game the previous Thursday and the match got under way in a blustery wind. Barber hit the post with a snap shot after only five minutes and then three minutes later Vale went ahead, Askey crossing for Cunliffe to head into the corner of the net.

The Mariners equalised after 27 minutes when Fred Smith headed home, but Vale regained the lead six minutes later, Sproson and Leake's interpassing ending with the latter hitting a low shot past Harry Nicholson in the Grimsby goal. The home side equalised again with another header, this time from Jimmy Hernon. Vale went in with the score 2-2 at half time for the only time in the season. The second half saw several chances but no further scoring in what was described as Blundell Park's best game of the season.

Vale – King, Turner, Potts, Mullard, Cheadle, Sproson, Askey, Tomkinson, Barber, Leake, Cunliffe
Att: 9,952

On the same day Oxford won the 100th boat race.

Monday 5 April

**Port Vale 1 Mansfield Town 1**

Ken Griffiths returned in place of Tomkinson but rain had left the pitch in its worst state of the season and the midfield was almost unplayable. This resulted in the game being a sluggish, grim affair. Cheadle and Barber picked up injuries and then Mansfield took the lead a minute before half-time when outside-left Alan Daley hit a low shot just inside the post. The second half began in sleet, which continued throughout, and Cheadle played on the wing because of his injury. Vale equalised after 59 minutes, Barber shooting home after a through ball by Sproson, and Cunliffe later hit the post, but the Valiants had to settle for another draw.

Vale – King, Turner, Potts, Mullard, Cheadle, Sproson, Askey, Leake, Barber, Griffiths, Cunliffe
Att: 13,060

**Bradford City 1 Port Vale 1**

Cheadle was out injured with the pulled thigh muscle he had sustained in the game on the previous Monday and Turner was missing for only the second time in the season. Griffiths was also out again. In addition, Hayward hadn't played since the semi-final and, despite being back in training, wasn't yet ready to play. After 19 minutes George Williamson hit a shot through a pack of players to give Bradford the lead, then Barber and Askey had to leave the field temporarily for attention to knocks.

Vale began the second half well on top but equalised somewhat fortuitously after 59 minutes when Askey's cross was missed by the Bradford 'keeper Geoff Smith and dropped into the corner of the net.

Vale – King, Elsby, Potts, Mullard, Sproson, Leake, Askey, Tomkinson, Barber, Cunliffe, Hulligan
Att: 15,240

Tommy Cheadle's injury must have been a bad one to keep him out of the game as it was often said of him that instead of the black and white colours of the Vale shirt he would have been better off in black and blue – because that was the colour of his knees after a game.

Tommy himself said: "I played the game hard, but never squealed. I remember once at Brighton having stitches put in a gash and going straight back into the match. I also had an injection on the touchline once so I could stay in a game."

Colleagues remarked: "It was not a game for Tommy – it was war."

Thursday 8 April

Ray King was included in a list of 32 players under consideration for England's two full internationals against Yugoslavia in Belgrade and Hungary in Budapest and two 'B' internationals against Yugoslavia in Zagreb and Greece 'B' in Athens. He was the only third division player named and said "It is a great honour and has come as a thrilling surprise. I feel that it is not only a personal reward, but a recognition of the Vale's wonderful defensive record in league and cup this season. It is a tribute to my team-mates as much as to me, for I owe a lot to them."

It was announced that, in the event of a draw in the FA Cup final on Saturday 1 May, there would be a replay at Goodison Park the following Wednesday at 6:30pm.

Saturday 10 April

**Port Vale 7 Stockport County 0**

This was the Vale's seventh game in a fortnight, eighth if the All Stars testimonial match is included, but any fatigue didn't show as they achieved their biggest win of the season! Turner returned at right-back and Hayward led the attack for the first time since the FA Cup semi-final, but Cheadle and Griffiths were still injured.

Hayward opened the scoring after eight minutes with a shot from outside the penalty area and he added the second 11 minutes later after Tomkinson had hit the post. It was 3-0 after 25 minutes when Askey scored with a low drive and then, as if making up for lost time after his two week absence, Hayward completed a 23 minute hat-trick when, in the 31$^{st}$ minute, he hooked the ball into the net while still on the ground following a tussle! Incredibly it was five a minute later when Askey hammered home his second of the game and then six after 36 minutes as Cunliffe netted with a carefully aimed shot.

Halfway through the second half Vale completed the scoring when Tomkinson headed home a cross from Askey. Vale now only needed a maximum of four points from their last six games to be certain of being champions even if their rivals won all their remaining matches.

Vale – King, Turner, Potts, Mullard, Sproson, Leake, Askey, Tomkinson, Hayward, Cunliffe, Bennett
Att: 19,513

The six goal lead at half time is still a club record.

Crook Town and Bishop Auckland drew 2-2 at Wembley in the Amateur Cup final in front of a crowd of 100,000. The tie went to two replays before Crook won 1-0 in the third game.

<u>Monday 12 April</u>

Bill Haley and the Comets recorded 'Rock Around the Clock'. The current number one in the hit parade was "Secret Love" by Doris Day, which she also sang in the film Calamity Jane.

<u>Wednesday 14 April</u>

The annual match between School and Old Boys marking the end of Easter Term took place at Hanley High School. Vale's Roy Brien was the referee and Ray Hancock and Alan Bennett were the linesmen.

<u>Thursday 15 April</u>

After their brief rest, Vale were to play three games in four days over Easter with matches on Good Friday, Easter Saturday and Easter Monday, all of which were to result in goalless draws. As at Christmas, the same opponents were faced twice; this time it was Southport, who Vale had previously met in the FA Cup in December.

<u>Friday 16 April</u>

**Port Vale 0 Southport 0**

The first of the Easter games was unrewarding fare for the bumper holiday crowd of almost 27,000 who had turned up to watch. Cheadle, Griffiths and Hayward were once again out injured. Vale's best efforts came from Barber and Bennett, while Sproson injured his shoulder but played on. Southport 'keeper Ray Minshull made two good saves near the end as Vale came close to a winning goal.

Vale – King, Turner, Potts, Mullard, Sproson, Leake, Askey, Tomkinson, Barber, Cunliffe, Bennett
Att: 26,941

<u>Saturday 17 April</u>

**Rochdale 0 Port Vale 0**

Vale clinched the Championship of Division Three (North) and promotion to Division 2 despite being forced to make further drastic

126

team changes at Spotland. Sproson's injured shoulder kept him out and, as Cheadle was still injured, Leake took over at centre-half and 20 year-old Roy Brien was brought in for his debut. Brien had become a full-time professional just before Christmas 1953 on the completion of his national service with the RAF. It was to be his only ever Football League game!

The Dale had the better of the first half without really coming close to scoring. There was an ironic incident, given what had happened three weeks previously at Villa Park, when, halfway through the second half, Askey put Barber through and he looked to be tripped well inside the penalty area but the referee gave a free-kick just outside!

Vale – King, Turner, Potts, Mullard, Leake, Brien, Askey, Tomkinson, Barber, Cunliffe, Bennett
Att: 14,749

Monday 19 April

**Southport 0 Port Vale 0**

Sproson, Griffiths and Hayward returned, but the Vale team was still not at full strength because Elsby had to come in for Turner and Leake continued at centre-half as Cheadle was still out injured. It was a gloriously sunny Bank Holiday at the seaside, and Champions Port Vale wore red and white stripes as they had in the cup-tie at Haig Avenue earlier in the season. The game was much better than the one on Good Friday but also finished without a goal. Hayward had an effort cleared off the line and Minshull made a good save from Tomkinson in Vale's best efforts.

Vale – King, Elsby, Potts, Mullard, Leake, Sproson, Askey, Tomkinson, Hayward, Griffiths, Cunliffe
Att: 12,328

Thursday 22 April

It was announced that Vale would be presented with the Division Three (North) Championship Shield at Saturday's home game with Wrexham and that there would be a souvenir edition of the club programme in commemoration, costing double the usual price at 6d (two and a half pence).

Goalkeeper Ray King was named in the 31 man England squad for the forthcoming tour to Yugoslavia and Hungary.

Freddie Steele and Tommy Cheadle appeared on the 'Sportsview' programme on TV that evening.

<u>Friday 23 April</u>

Vale retained the Sentinel Shield by beating Stoke Boys Club 2-0 at the Victoria Ground in Stoke. Captain Ken Higgs scored the first goal from the penalty spot and Ray Askey, Colin's brother, scored the second from a corner.

<u>Saturday 24 April</u>

Vale were the only club in the whole Football League not to lose a home game so far in the 1953/54 season and wanted to maintain that distinction. Before that game, an informal luncheon was held at the George Hotel in Burslem where the club's Chairman FW Burgess described Vale's season as a football fairy story come true. Mr AH Oakley JP, senior Vice-President of the Football League and President of the Staffordshire FA, was present at the lunch and would be presenting the Championship Shield after the game.

**Port Vale 2 Wrexham 0**

With Turner and Cheadle returning Vale were back to full strength for their first home game since clinching the title. It was the first time that the Vale had been at full strength since the cup-tie at Leyton Orient, 12 games ago. The first half was fairly even but Cheadle's thigh injury recurred leaving him limping. In the second half Vale laid siege to the Wrexham goal but were unlucky after 53 minutes when Leake headed Cunliffe's centre onto the bar and then also headed the rebound onto the bar and over! The first goal arrived two minutes later; Tommy Cheadle centred the ball into the box where it was knocked out to Albert Mullard. He slipped it to Colin Askey and his cross was subsequently headed home by Ken Griffiths.

Twenty minutes from time Wrexham's Ally McGowan limped off the field with what turned out to be a broken collar bone, so they carried on with ten men as substitutes were still over ten years away.

Vale made the game safe in the 74<sup>th</sup> minute with their second goal. Basil Hayward hit a crossfield pass to Dickie Cunliffe and he hit

128

a shot that was blocked by Phil Spruce. The rebound came back to Cunliffe and he made no mistake the second time.

Vale – King, Turner, Potts, Mullard, Cheadle, Sproson, Askey, Leake, Hayward, Griffiths, Cunliffe
Att: 18,174

As the final whistle blew, hundreds of boys led the crowds which swarmed onto the pitch for the presentation of the Championship Shield. It was presented to Tommy Cheadle by Mr Oakley who was also chairman of Wolverhampton Wanderers, who had just won the First Division title, with West Brom finishing in second place.

A huge roar went up for the presentation, the second time the Vale had won it, 1930 being the previous occasion. Chairman Fred Burgess and manager Freddie Steele also addressed the crowd. Steele said, "My unhappiest moment of the season was after the FA Cup semi-final, as the players' hearts were set on playing at Wembley. Their disappointment was something I didn't want to see again. But this is my proudest moment - Port Vale have no player who can be singled out for special praise; the title was won by 11 players who all gave their best and the credit is shared equally by the whole team."

Tom Finney was named as the Football Writers Footballer of the Year.

Halifax and Warrington drew 4-4 in the Rugby League Challenge Cup Final at Wembley, the only time there have been no tries in the Challenge Cup Final. Warrington won the replay 8-4 at Odsal Stadium, Bradford on 5 May in front of a record crowd of 102,569!

Monday 26 April

**Stockport County 1 Port Vale 1**

Albert Leake missed the game with a groin strain so Derek Tomkinson took his place.

Stockport were still smarting from the 7-0 mauling they had at Vale Park so took no prisoners with their challenges. In the 10th minute Ray Weigh hit the bar, but Tommy Cheadle cleared the rebound. Ray King produced a marvellous save on the half-hour mark from David Herd to keep the scoreline blank. Herd went on to score in the FA Cup final for Man United and also played for Stoke.

Vale took the lead in the 39<sup>th</sup> minute with virtually their first effort on goal. Basil Hayward backheeled a Stan Turner throw in to Colin Askey and he squared it to Dickie Cunliffe who fired the ball home past former Stoke 'keeper Dennis Herod.

In the 57<sup>th</sup> minute Ken Griffiths was carried off on a stretcher after a collision with George Pilkington. He came back on after a few minutes but could not carry on and he eventually had to spend the night in hospital with concussion. Stockport levelled eleven minutes from time. Allen Oliver chipped the ball into the box and Weigh scrambled it home.

Vale – King, Turner, Potts, Mullard, Cheadle, Sproson, Askey, Tomkinson, Hayward, Griffiths, Cunliffe
Att: 11,840

## Wednesday 28 April

Despite such a busy end to the season, Ray King, Reg Potts and Roy Sproson played in a fund raising game for the Staffs County FA, lining up for the Staffs XI v Stoke City at the Victoria Ground. Stoke won 4-1; it was the only time King had conceded more than two in a game all season!

Vale retained the Sentinel Cup by defeating Stoke Boys Club 3-0 in front of a crowd of 2,500 at Vale Park. The Vale goals came from Higgs (penalty), Moran and Shaw.

Ken Griffiths had returned home from hospital but had to rest for a couple of days so would have to miss the final game of the season v Darlington.

## Thursday 29 April

**Port Vale 1 Darlington 1**

Vale went into the game just needing to avoid conceding four goals to set up a new defensive record for the Football League since it was extended in 1919. Tommy Cheadle missed the game as well as Griffiths, with Albert Leake coming in at centre half and Alan Bennett wide on the left.

Vale started sluggishly and fell a goal behind after 18 minutes. Harry Houlahan chipped a Leake clearance into the danger area, John Dowson nodded it down and Jim French shot home. On the half hour mark Vale almost drew level when a Basil Hayward shot cannoned off 'keeper Billy Dunn's legs before Joe Devlin, lying on the line, just managed to get his leg to the ball and divert it away.

George Wardle limped off in the 41$^{st}$ minute reducing the Quakers to ten men and a minute later Vale equalised. Alan Bennett sent a cross over from the left and Derek Tomkinson rose to head the ball home.

Vale – King, Turner, Potts, Mullard, Leake, Sproson, Askey, Tomkinson, Hayward, Cunliffe, Bennett
Att: 11,052

Vale conceded only 21 goals in 46 league games. The next best defence in the whole Football League was Blackburn Rovers who conceded 50 in 42 games in Division 2. The next best defence in Division 3(North) was shared between Gateshead and Bradford City who each conceded 55 league goals.

Vale won the title by 11 points which was the biggest ever winning margin at that time.

Vale played 54 competitive games in the season, which no English team had ever done before,and they were unbeaten in 50 of them!

Vale only conceded 26 goals in those 54 games, conceding two goals six times, one goal 13 times and keeping 35 clean sheets. Their 4 defeats were 2-0, 2-1, 2-1 and 1-0.

Vale kept 30 clean sheets in the league, which is still a Football League record today. Ray King kept 29 of them, also a record at the time, since only equalled by Gillingham's Jim Stannard in 1995/96.

Six of Vale's eight FA Cup-ties were refereed by Yorkshiremen, four by referees from Leeds. The first round tie at Darlington and the semi-final at Villa Park were both refereed by Mr H Webb from Leeds, and Vale's second round tie at Southport and the final between West Brom and Preston were both refereed by Mr. AW Luty from Leeds!

60 years on, eight of the grounds Vale played at in 1953/54 don't exist any more:

Peel Park, Accrington
Park Avenue, Bradford PA
Ninian Park, Cardiff
Sealand Road, Chester
Saltergate, Chesterfield
Feethams, Darlington
Redheugh Park, Gateshead and
The Old Show Ground, Scunthorpe.


60 years later 13 of the teams in Div 3(N) in 53/54 are currently in the Football League:
Accrington, Barnsley, Bradford City, Carlisle, Chesterfield, Crewe Alex, Hartlepool, Mansfield T, Port Vale, Rochdale, Scunthorpe U, Tranmere R and York C.
11 are now non-league:
Barrow, Bradford PA, Chester, Darlington, Gateshead, Grimsby T, Halifax T, Southport, Stockport Co, Workington and Wrexham.

Final table:

|  | P | W | D | L | F | A | PTS |
|---|---|---|---|---|---|---|---|
| PORT VALE | 46 | 26 | 17 | 3 | 74 | 21 | 69 |
| Barnsley | 46 | 24 | 10 | 12 | 77 | 57 | 58 |
| Scunthorpe Utd | 46 | 21 | 15 | 10 | 77 | 56 | 57 |
| Gateshead | 46 | 21 | 13 | 12 | 74 | 55 | 55 |
| Bradford City | 46 | 22 | 9 | 15 | 60 | 55 | 53 |
| Chesterfield | 46 | 19 | 14 | 13 | 76 | 64 | 52 |
| Mansfield T | 46 | 20 | 11 | 15 | 88 | 67 | 51 |
| Wrexham | 46 | 21 | 9 | 16 | 81 | 68 | 51 |
| Bradford P A | 46 | 18 | 14 | 14 | 77 | 68 | 50 |
| Stockport Co | 46 | 18 | 11 | 17 | 77 | 67 | 47 |
| Southport | 46 | 17 | 12 | 17 | 63 | 60 | 46 |
| Barrow | 46 | 16 | 12 | 18 | 72 | 71 | 44 |
| Carlisle Utd | 46 | 14 | 15 | 17 | 83 | 71 | 43 |
| Tranmere R | 46 | 18 | 7 | 21 | 59 | 70 | 43 |
| Accrington S | 46 | 16 | 10 | 20 | 66 | 74 | 42 |
| Crewe Alex | 46 | 14 | 13 | 19 | 49 | 67 | 41 |
| Grimsby T | 46 | 16 | 9 | 21 | 51 | 77 | 41 |
| Hartlepools Utd | 46 | 13 | 14 | 19 | 59 | 65 | 40 |
| Rochdale | 46 | 15 | 10 | 21 | 59 | 77 | 40 |
| Workington | 46 | 13 | 14 | 19 | 59 | 80 | 40 |
| Darlington | 46 | 12 | 14 | 20 | 50 | 71 | 38 |
| York  City | 46 | 12 | 13 | 21 | 64 | 86 | 37 |
| Halifax Town | 46 | 12 | 10 | 24 | 44 | 73 | 34 |
| Chester | 46 | 11 | 10 | 25 | 48 | 67 | 32 |

Vale's home and away league breakdown:

|  | P | W | D | L | F | A | PTS |
|---|---|---|---|---|---|---|---|
| Home | 23 | 16 | 7 | 0 | 48 | 5 | 39 |
| Away | 23 | 10 | 10 | 3 | 26 | 16 | 30 |

Vale's breakdown for all games:

|  | P | W | D | L | F | A |
|---|---|---|---|---|---|---|
| Home | 25 | 18 | 7 | 0 | 52 | 5 |
| Away | 29 | 14 | 11 | 4 | 35 | 20 |
| Total | 54 | 32 | 18 | 4 | 87 | 25 |

Average home attendance – 16,653. It was a club record at the time, since only being beaten in 1954/55 (20,869) and 1955/56 (18,985).

Appearances/goalscorers;

League Apps;

46 – Mullard
45 – Askey, King, Sproson
43 – Turner
42 – Cunliffe, Potts
40 – Leake
38 – Cheadle
37 – Hayward
36 – Griffiths
19 – Tomkinson
8 – Barber
7 – Elsby
5 – Bennett, Hulligan
1 – Brien, Hancock, Lewis

Scorers;

22 - Hayward
16 - Griffiths
13 - Leake
8  - Cunliffe
5 – Askey, Tomkinson
2 – Barber, Sproson
1 - Mullard

FA Cup Apps

8 - Askey, Cheadle, Cunliffe,
   Hayward, King, Leake,
   Mullard, Potts, Sproson,
   Turner
7 - Griffiths
1 - Tomkinson

Scorers;

7 - Leake
3 - Hayward
1 – Askey, Cunliffe, Griffiths

Backrow - Bill Cope (asst trainer), Mullard, Turner, Sproson, King, Hayward, Potts. Tomkinson
Third row - N Jones (secretary), LP Droy (director), W Elkes (director), Alderman G. L Barber (director), A McMinn (director), Alderman
William A Holdcroft (vice-chairman), F Pinfold (director), J Machin (director), J Diffin (director), LParton (groundsman)
Second row: Freddie Steele (manager), Askey, Hulligan, Leake, Fred Burgess (chairman), Cheadle, Griffiths, Cunliffe, Ken Fish (trainer)
Front row - Barber, Elsby, Bennett, Brien

135

LEYTON ORIENT FOOTBALL CLUB LTD.
LEYTON STADIUM, E.10
**Covered Stand** STANDING ONLY
OLIVER ROAD ENTRANCE
Price **5/-** inc. Tax Nº **8086**
FOOTBALL ASSOCIATION CUP (Round 6)
**LEYTON ORIENT**
v.
**PORT VALE**
SATURDAY, 13th MARCH, 1954
KICK-OFF 3.0 p.m.
A. H. R. HUGGETT, Secretary
■ YOU ARE ADVISED TO COME EARLY ■
Grove Press E.10 THIS PORTION TO BE RETAINED

Nº 46345
Aston Villa Football Club Ltd.
Saturday, March 27th, 1954
**F.A. CUP SEMI-FINAL**
At VILLA PARK BIRMINGHAM. KICK-OFF 3 p.m.
**W.B. ALBION** v. **PORT VALE**
Ground Admission Ticket **2/6** Including Tax
**Entrance Block** **A** **WITTON LANE**
Secretary.
ASTON VILLA F.C. Ltd.

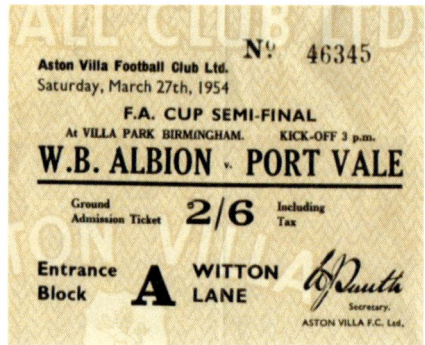

**Tickets for the two of the biggest FA Cup ties in Vale's history**

**Tommy Cheadle's bar at the Hamil End of the ground, a lasting legacy to Tommy**

136

**Details of special trains to Villa Park for the semi-final.**

**The bowl given to all players and staff to commemorate the club's achievements**

**Ray King, still in his goalkeeper's jersey 60 years on, living in Thailand**

# May

West Brom won the FA Cup Final, beating Preston North End 3-2 at Wembley Stadium. Ronnie Allen scored two of Albion's goals, including another penalty. The Vale team were in the crowd at Wembley that day. Ray King said: "The club took us down to watch the final as a bit of a treat. Our hearts weren't really in it though and I didn't think it was that great a game. Every player knew it should have been us."

The retained list was announced, with all senior professionals being retained. Four young professionals were freed, Cook, Viggars, Jones and Lovatt whilst Wharton was placed on the open to transfer list.

Monday 3 May

The Vale youngsters won the Staffs County Youth Cup beating Wolves 2-1 in the final at the Old Recreation Ground in Hanley. That was where Vale played their first team games up until moving to Vale Park in 1950. Wolves had won the cup the previous four years and took the lead, but goals from Pierpoint and Donaldson turned the game in Vale's favour. Ken Higgs also missed a penalty.

Wednesday 5 May

A banquet was held in honour of Vale's achievements at the Jubilee Hall, part of the Town Hall, in Stoke. All of the players and staff were presented with commemorative pottery bowls with facsimiles of all the directors, players and staff signatures on them. The only player not at the banquet was Ray King who was away with the England squad, the only time that has happened in the club's history!

The Lord Mayor, Alderman AE Bennett, said that it was a fantastic achievement. When he took office he proclaimed that Vale would win the league and that Stoke City would be promoted to Division One – one out of two wasn't bad!

On the same evening, Vale featured heavily in a recorded radio programme called 'Top Honours', broadcast only in the Midlands where football personalities looked back over the season. Freddie Steele, Tommy Cheadle, and Basil Hayward all contributed.

Freddie Steele attributed the close-knit camaraderie and togetherness of the squad to the fact that the majority of the players were married. He said, "It is much harder to control a group of single men in their early 20's - married ones have responsibilities and behave far better."

Of the first choice line up nine were married, Dickie Cunliffe was due to marry in June 1954 and Basil Hayward was engaged to Stoke player Roy Beckett's sister.

**The players sign autographs for dancers at the Queens Theatre, Burslem**

<u>Thursday 6 May</u>

Vale announced that they would be flying to Ireland for a short three game tour on 12$^{th}$ May, returning on the 20$^{th}$. Two games would be in Southern Ireland and one would be in the North. They had also been offered tours to Belgium and France, but chose the Irish option.

Roger Bannister became the first man to run a mile in under 4 minutes, clocking a time of 3 minutes, 59.4 seconds at Oxford.

## Wednesday 12 May

Vale duly flew to Ireland for their post season tour, the only player missing being Ray King, who was on international duty.

Colin Askey said, "We were kitted out in new blazers and trousers and promised a sum of money for 'expenses'. We had just had a great season and deserved a bit of a celebratory wind down. The club agreed to a sum of money for each of us, but would only give us half of it in advance, with the other half to come during the tour."

## Friday 14 May

The first game of the Vale's tour was against a Shelbourne XI at Dalymount Park, Dublin. The Shelbourne team only had one Shelbourne player in it, the goalkeeper according to Ray Hancock, and included many stars from the English game including Jimmy Hill, the future Coventry manager and TV pundit, Johnny Haynes the Fulham player, Bobby Robson the future England manager, John Charles, the Welsh striker and Charlie Mitten, formerly of Manchester United. Charles' brother Mel went on to play 7 games for the Vale in the 1960's.

In the event Vale won 4-1 with Albert Leake scoring a hat trick and Basil Hayward notching the other one. Vale director Jack Diffin was a former goalkeeper with Shelbourne in the 1930's.

Goalkeeper Ray Hancock said, "The Shelbourne goal was a foul really, Jimmy Hill just bundled me over the line. It was a good trip and we went on a trip to Blarney Castle where we all had to kiss the Blarney Stone."

## Sunday 16 May

The second game of the Irish tour took place at Cork City where Vale won 3-1, John Charles again playing against the Vale as a guest. The scorers were Dickie Cunliffe, Ken Griffiths and Basil Hayward. It was a double celebration for Griffiths as his wife gave birth to a daughter on the same day!

Ken said, "My job was a professional footballer, so when the club said I would be required to go on tour to Ireland there was no question of me not going despite Nancy's (his wife's) condition."

The Cork programme welcomed Vale by saying 'Congratulations to Port Vale who had a terrific run to the semi-finals of the FA Cup, defeating Cardiff City, Blackpool and Stoke City on the way.' That would certainly have put the icing on the cake!

Roy Sproson remembered, "After the 1953-54 promotion season we went on a tour of Ireland and there we became involved in what I call the "Battle of Cork." We had previously beaten a Representative XI 4-1 in Dublin and animosity was stacked against us.
Nevertheless, Manager Freddie Steele instructed us to take it easy until the home side started to kick chunks out of us and led 1-0 at halftime. I had my eye split. Freddie then told us to "let 'em have it" and they hardly knew what had hit them. They had bitten off more than they could chew and we won 3-1 in the end."

On the same evening Ray King was on the substitute's bench for the full England team for their game against Yugoslavia in Belgrade. England lost 1-0 but Ray remained on the bench. It remains the closest any Vale player has ever got to representing England in a full international.

### Monday 17 May

The fixtures for the 1954/55 season were released for Vale's first appearance in the Second Division for 18 years. There was also the spice of league games against Stoke City for the first time in 21 years.

### Wednesday 19 May

Vale's tour finished on a high with a 5-2 victory at Glenavon, a game which also doubled up as Billy Cush's testimonial. The scorers were Dickie Cunliffe (2), Colin Askey, Micky Hulligan and Basil Hayward.

### Thursday 20 May

Colin Askey takes up the rest of the story of the Irish trip. "There was no sign of the other half of the money we had all been promised since we set off on the trip so we asked Freddie Steele about it. We deserved it, because we had had a great season and also won all our games on the Irish tour so we fulfilled our side of the bargain. Freddie went to the directors, but they said they couldn't afford it, the money had run out!

In the end we had to return to England by boat, the club hadn't even got the money for the flight home!"

The story never made the press, and no fuss was made. There would have been hell to pay had it happened 60 years later!

<u>Saturday 22 May</u>

Ray King made his England debut for the 'B' team away to Switzerland in Basle. Two other former Vale players were also in the side, Bill McGarry and Ronnie Allen, the latter having destroyed Vale's cup final hopes two months earlier. Ray was substituted at half time with England losing 1-0 and eventually they lost 2-0.

That was the end of the season. Profits were £2,628, wages had risen £11,000 from the previous year to £50,940, whilst transfer fees received were £350. Ground improvements had cost £5,628 during the season. For the Vale ahead lay an assault on the second division and a renewal of the rivalry with Stoke City on an even keel.

A further celebratory banquet was held at the Grand Hotel in Hanley on 3 June at which championship medals were presented to Freddie Steele and Ken Fish.

Perhaps the last word about the 'Men of Steele' is best left to Roy Sproson, the Vale's longest-serving player, who said: "They were a grand bunch of players and nearly all local-born with pride in their hearts to play for Port Vale."